With the Sun in My Eyes

The story of Char Sundust, psychic healer and shamanic practitioner

Mikaya Heart

iUniverse, Inc.
New York Bloomington

With the Sun in My Eyes

The story of Char Sundust, psychic healer and shamanic practitioner

Copyright © 2008 by Mikaya Heart

All rights reserved. No part of this book may be used or reproduced by any means, graphic, electronic, or mechanical, including photocopying, recording, taping or by any information storage retrieval system without the written permission of the publisher except in the case of brief quotations embodied in critical articles and reviews.

iUniverse books may be ordered through booksellers or by contacting:

iUniverse
1663 Liberty Drive
Bloomington, IN 47403
www.iuniverse.com
1-800-Authors (1-800-288-4677)

Because of the dynamic nature of the Internet, any Web addresses or links contained in this book may have changed since publication and may no longer be valid. The views expressed in this work are solely those of the author and do not necessarily reflect the views of the publisher, and the publisher hereby disclaims any responsibility for them.

ISBN: 978-0-595-51203-4 (pbk)
ISBN: 978-0-595-50733-7 (cloth)
ISBN: 978-0-595-61800-2 (ebk)

Printed in the United States of America

iUniverse rev. date: 12/29/2008

This book must be dedicated to:

The Earth that we inhabit
This Blue-water World
This extra-special planet

Acknowledgments

My heartfelt gratitude goes to Char herself, of course, and to all the wonderful people who allowed me to interview them, most particularly: Claudia, Lawrence, Storme, Sally, Barbara, Matilda, Pam, Cougar Woman, Lena, Joy, and all of Ben's family; also to Kay who did some great editing for me.

Thank you!

I must also acknowledge my teachers. In singling out some names, I find that every being I meet is my teacher. Here are a few of them: my father, Martine Standish, Maggie Norton, Jesse Cougar, Cindy Evans, Brooke Medicine Eagle, Laura Rose, Caryn McClosky, Angeles Arrien, Dayana Jon and AMAG.

And last, but certainly not least: Joey, Jake and Growler, every flower, tree, leaf, and rock, every drop of water, every breath of air, every cloud and every star, all that we call Mother Nature, everything that has held me and nurtured me and loved me unconditionally, wiping away my tears and washing my heart.

Preface

I met Char Sundust in 1998. Spirit had already told her that she should write a book, and when she realized that I am a writer, she asked for my help. Since my writing style is very different from Char's, our attempts to produce a book together didn't work, but by the time I had followed Char around for a year or two, and interviewed dozens of her friends and clients, as well as family members, I was inspired to write the book you have in your hands. I have spun together dozens of threads provided by different people; the earlier years of her life are partially fictionalized to make the story readable, to round out the facts that were relayed to me by Char herself, her mother and her brothers. From Chapter Six onwards, the healing work described is all in the recent past, and the facts were gleaned from Char herself and others who were present. I have included my own perspective when it is appropriate, since I drummed for Char on a number of her healing journeys. Although I am not able to see the things seen by shamanic healers who work outside the physical arena, I could both see and feel the effects of Char's actions in those other realms.

Some may complain that I present Char as too perfect. My response is that, as a healer, her integrity is unimpeachable. I have no misgivings about recommending her as a practitioner and teacher. As a regular human being, outside of her work, she has the same issues as many others. This book is about her and her work, not her private life. I have represented her as fairly and truthfully as I am able.

Other people have wanted a workbook, something that is more specifically a teaching tool. While I fully acknowledge the importance of such books, one of the most reliable methods of learning is through a good story. It was not hard to produce a good story about someone as remarkable and inspirational as Char.

Some of Char's teachers used the terms *shaman* and *medicine woman* to describe her and what she was doing. These days, those terms are loaded with implications of cultural misappropriation. Unfortunately, white Western culture has very little history of shamanic methods of healing, so we don't have traditional words to describe them. Searching for the right terminology is an ongoing task, getting slowly easier as more people are acknowledging the validity of this kind of healing. I hope that this book will play its part in the process of education. Please know that I have not intended to offend anyone.

On the following page is a brief glossary of words that may be unfamiliar to those readers who have not studied shamanism.

Glossary

Ally: any being (alive or dead, in this realm or in another realm) that assists in shamanic work for the higher good of all.

Chanupa: the sacred pipe, used in some Native American tribes. Specific people, often shamans or medicine people, are designated pipe carriers, and are in charge of the chanupa.

Clairsentience: the ability to become aware of things in non-physical realms through feeling.

Clairvoyance: the ability to become aware of things in non-physical realms through seeing images.

Drum journey: using the sound of the drum to transport oneself to another realm of consciousness.

Entity: a piece of energy that is concentrated enough to appear to be a conscious being of some variety.

Power animal: the spirit of an animal that has strong affinity with a particular person, and acts as a guide or ally for her/him. Usually it is not a particular individual animal, rather it is the energy of that species.

Psychopomp: to assist a spirit who has died to move on from the land of the living.

Schmutz: a slang term referring to undesirable stray pieces of energy that get stuck to people or things.

Smudge: sage, cedar or other herbs that are used to clean the energy of objects, people, or places. They may be burnt to produce cleansing smoke.

Realm: an arena of consciousness, as in, *the physical realm*, *the astral realm*. There are many realms. We don't have names for most of them, because most of us are unaware of their existence.

Wicca: the ancient Celtic religion based on witchcraft.

Prologue

Char's home was a downstairs apartment, overhung by a large cedar at the front, on 12th Ave in the University District of Seattle. As soon as you walked in the door, you were surrounded by sweet singing energy. Crystals, bones, rocks and feathers sat on shelves and tables to left and right. A small dog with a very long nose and very happy energy greeted all newcomers enthusiastically, while cats inspected everyone more carefully from a distance.

Because she was a close friend and associate of Char's, I had requested a meeting with Carol, also known as Cougar Woman. We sat in the front room talking about the trip they had taken together, while Char went to look for photos.

"When Char called me up and asked if I would come to Japan with her to lead sweat lodges, I wasn't sure, because although I have been to a lot of sweats, I've never led any in this country, and I am mostly white, so it is clearly not appropriate for me to teach Native American methods. But I've done sweats according to a number of different traditions, and my favorite was led by a Nesquali woman. She said, the sweat is for purification before other ceremonies, or it can stand alone, and it *is* what you bring into it. I liked that philosophy.

"So I thought and prayed for a week, and then I decided it would be OK for me to go and teach about the purpose behind the sweat lodge, and the background on it, as long as I always made it clear that I was doing it for them to claim as their own process, not in the traditional way. So I decided to go."

"Yeah, and it was phenomenal, the sweats were divine," Char called from the other room, where she was leafing through drawers.

"Why are the Japanese so interested in Native American spirituality? How did they come to hear about Char?" I asked.

"I don't know why they are so interested in Native American stuff. There was always a language barrier and so there were a lot of questions I never really got an answer to, but I think they'd been introduced to it by the Bear Tribe, who do a lot of international work. There were a couple of other Westerners, from the Bear Tribe, who were there at the same time, although we barely met them."

Char came walking in from the other room, holding a bundle of photos. "I met the Japanese people when I did a gourd ceremony with my Lakota mom, Barbara Means Adams, at the Love and Light Foundation. So then they invited me to go over there. They paid for everything, it was wonderful."

"Yes, it was amazing," Carol agreed. "It must be the one of the few times in my life when I didn't have to think about where my meals were going to come from for two whole weeks. We always knew there was going to be food around the corner and a bed to sleep in, and all we have to do is share what we know, and do healing work. I didn't think about anything except why I was there. I was just in spirit the whole time, on cloud nine."

It occurred to me that cloud nine is probably a good description of the state Char inhabits on a daily basis.

Carol continued. "But let me start at the beginning. Traveling with Char, as you can imagine, is a whole trip in itself. You just *do* it, you have to *not* care what anyone else is thinking, because she doesn't care, and she isn't *going* to care. So we're in line waiting to get on the plane, and she smiles at someone, and says, 'That is such a beautiful dress, such wonderful colors!' Or something like that, you know how she is." We all laughed, Char loudest of all.

"Anyway she got into a conversation, and they asked her why she was going to Japan, so she told them she was a psychic. The plane had no sooner taken off than one of the stewardesses came up to ask Char if she would give readings to them during their breaks. So she spent the whole ten hour trip giving readings to the stewardesses, in the smoking section at the back of the plane. And I was doing my leather work, so I had this huge long strip of leather laid out on the seats. Then towards the end of the flight there was this little Filipino gal, and you could just tell she was in distress. She came up to me and she asked, 'are you the psychic?' So I said, 'no, that's Char, she is sitting right here.' Well, the plane was getting ready to land, and she didn't have any money, but she really needed some help so Char gave her a reading. I was sitting next to them, tuning all this out, carefully not listening."

Char interjected, "Yeah, you managed that really well." She was enjoying Carol's narrative, smiling and chuckling to herself.

"Yes, I did! Well, the plane lands and the Filipino gal still has all these questions. Everyone else is getting off the plane, and Char is still answering questions. She's oblivious to the fact that the plane has emptied, and there might be people waiting for us, so I just don't care either, I *have to not care*, so I don't, I'm just sitting there tuning out my worries, tuning out Char and the woman she is reading. Finally the stewardesses managed to herd us off the plane.

"Well, the amazing thing is that when we got on the plane to go home two weeks later, this Filipino woman is on the same plane. So, of course she greets us, 'Char, Char, everything was just like you said it would be!' That was really cool, to get confirmation like that, after giving someone something and seeing what they do with it, seeing that it all worked out. And she seemed to be in a much better state, whatever it was all about had resolved somewhat. Of course I didn't know because I had so carefully not listened, but I could tell just looking at her that she was better."

Char turned towards me, beaming. "I was so grateful! And six months later she brought her whole family to me for readings. There were about twenty of them crammed into my little apartment, it was such fun."

Carol continued. "We were picked up at the airport, which is apparently fairly unheard of in Tokyo, people usually meet you at the train station. The drive from the airport to Mahdi's place was quite a ways. I remember it was dark when we got off the freeway, which they *don't* call a freeway—"

"*Not* free! Very expensive!" Char put on a Japanese speaker's accent. "We were having a blast just looking at everything: 'Oh, my god, there's a 7-Eleven!'" They both cracked up laughing.

"Mahdi is the Japanese woman who met us. Her son and her daughter were there. They fed us, and we did a pipe ceremony and then did this big exchange of gifts. They were so excited to see Char. Then we were supposed to be going up to Mame Isu where the people from the Bear Tribe were doing vision quest work, but we didn't go. We found out later the Bear Tribe people didn't want us there. Fortunately no one told us that until later."

"Yes, I'm really glad we didn't know that. We were supposed to be there for a full day while the Bear Tribe people were teaching. This gal from the Bear Tribe—" Char paused "—I won't say her name, I don't want to do any dishonoring here, but she asked that I not come. It was to do with my not being one hundred percent Native American. I am mostly white, but you know what? I don't pretend. I know who I am, I grew up immersed in traditional healing ways. None of that matters anyhow, it's what skill you carry with you now, and where your heart is! I felt like she just judged me without meeting me, and it was very hurtful. When we showed up, she wouldn't look at me, she wouldn't acknowledge my presence. I was very excited to meet her because she comes from a teacher I really respect and honor, Sun Bear. She just slammed me. I worked with it, I was OK with it. I still have a deep respect for Sun Bear; I know that people will do whatever they want to do with the teachings, and they don't necessarily walk the talk."

"So she's Native American?" I asked for clarification.

"Oh no, she's white! I wanted to say, hey lady, you're whiter than I am, and you haven't had any of the training I have, what are you going on about?" The last words burst out of her along with peals of laughter, then she was abruptly serious again. "Of course I would never say that, it would be totally inappropriate, it's just that I was very hurt." She shrugged sadly. "Anyway, there was a man, Richard, who was teaching with her, I really liked him. He was very sweet, and he related very openly with Carol and me. They left within half an hour of us getting there. At the time I dismissed it as unimportant, and to some degree I still do. But I feel passionately about it because it was not a good representation, it was not a good example for the people who were there, or for anyone."

"Have you experienced much of that kind of thing?" I asked. "I know I've seen it a lot: people who are doing spiritual and psychic work being competitive with each other, always vying with each other to show that they can do it better, and claiming to be more qualified."

"Oh yes, it's crazy, the competition between psychics," Char nodded vigorously, her eyes wide. "That's one of the reasons I started teaching a class. I use the archetypes as a tool to teach people how to get in touch with their psychic abilities, and how to use their psychic abilities with integrity. Most of the work in the class is intended to promote personal growth. There is a lot of journey work that is about connecting with your inner wisdom and following your heart. Basically the class is about how to be a better person, by using your intuition and your innate shamanic core gifts. Everybody has a shamanic background to *some* degree *somewhere*. Whatever that word *shamanic* means, we have such limited language in English, I don't know what other word to use. I try to teach my students about what there is beyond this physical world, about how to access that reality, and how to trust their instincts, and act honorably. Then if they choose to do psychic work, at least they're educated, they have some tools to work with."

"So have you been back to Japan since you went with Carol?"

"No, I've been invited several times, but I don't want to make any waves. There was a great big fight around all this, people were taking sides. I told Mahdi, don't fight about it, I'll come when it is time for me to come. I've stayed in touch with the Japanese people I met, they write me letters and send me photos when they want readings, or sometimes they will come over here. They came last year and had soul retrievals. They put me up in the Hilton in Spokane, and had me do readings there. That was a trip, I almost got kicked out of the Hilton twice. Five or six security guards turned up at the door, and here I am with this roomful of Japanese people, doing a gourd ceremony. The guards are all big and puffy, you know how they get, they are such twerps. They said, 'Ma'am, we're afraid we're going to have to ask you to stop whatever it is that you are doing!'"

She laughed, drawing deeply on her cigarette, and I leaned to the left, avoiding the smoke. She quickly turned her head to the side, blowing it away from me. "I wasn't even making much noise! We were sage-ing and rattling and singing. It was the smell of sage that flipped them out, I expect. The second time they came and said, 'We are going to have to physically remove you from the hotel, if you do not stop doing whatever it is you are doing.' I said, 'I think I rented this room, I think I am minding my own business!'"

I laughed at the image of Char smiling sweetly as she adamantly refused to back down.

"I told them I had a right to practice my spirituality. For Christ's sake, the Pope has condoned Native American religious practices! They left us alone after that. But usually the Japanese people would come only for a couple of days, and I would quite often stay up most of the night giving readings. One night I did readings from seven in the evening till six the next morning. But anyway!" She sat back in her seat, grinning at us. "Let's talk about being in Japan. We were just about to get to the bit where I pose as a rock star!" She slapped her leg as she cracked up.

"Oh yes," laughed Carol, "We went to this middle school and all these kids kept coming up to her, saying 'Are you a rock star? Are you a rock star?'" She mimicked a voice of awe. "And there was all this rock music blaring out throughout the school. We asked the English teacher, is it always like this? He said, 'No, it's their choice day, and they chose this rock music.' I guess they don't get to choose all the time, but that day they chose this, and they had it cranked up."

"But how come you went to a school? How did that get on the schedule?" I was a little bewildered.

Char grinned excitedly. "We asked if we could go! Mahdi's daughter was at that school, so we went at lunch time. I discovered later that it's unheard of, they don't let people in the schools."

Carol picked up the story. "Everywhere we went, Char was snatching at experience, whatever she could do. We were walking through some garden and there was an old woman picking kaki fruit, which is persimmon, so Char just walked up to her and said in her best sign language—because we didn't speak any Japanese, except for basics—" Char interrupted, reeling off a phrase in Japanese, which apparently means *thank you*. They both laughed again.

"I have a picture of Char on her tiptoes straining to pick this fruit, because they were really high up, and the old woman was helping her with a stick. Do you have that photo, Char? You should have that photo."

"No, I don't, I only have these here," she jabbed at the pile on her table with her cigarette.

"Then we went to a place that looked like southern California: tipis on the ocean overlooking the Pacific, very surreal. There was a bamboo forest…"

"Oh, the bamboo forest, that was so wonderful!"

"…and a U-pick shitake mushroom farm. I did two sweats there, while Char was doing readings. The Japanese were so loud in the sweats, they were banging rocks together and singing and drumming and rattling…"

"Yeah, I was doing readings on the porch, and I could clearly hear them. There was so much *joy*!"

"And they were singing, though of course I had no idea *what* they were singing, and people outside were *dancing*! We were all singing our own thing and it just all went together…"

"It was just *gorgeous*!" Char was laughing with the memory of it.

"…it was mostly vocal, it was loud, oh, man, I wished we had a tape recorder, because it was awesome. And this woman, Mahdi, she had the *best* energy. She was almost like Char, except she didn't quite have a handle on it, not that *she*'s got a handle on it either!"

She grinned at Char, whose infectious peals of laughter echoed round the room. "Yeah, right, what does *that* mean, having a handle on it!"

"It was amazing, I had never seen Char doing her thing, I had seen her at pipe circles and craft circles, but I had never seen her do her gourd ceremony before. She went round the circle with the rattle, and then people talked about what she had said to them, and the relationship between what she had said and what was really going on for them. It was like…wow! The looks on people's faces! They were all so amazed at what she saw. And then she would say, yeah, and you've got this going on for you too, and she would say something else astonishing. All this had to go through an interpreter, most of these people don't speak English."

"That poor interpreter! She was doing a great job, man, she *rocked*!"

"We learned how to prepare people for what was going to happen without having to stop every five seconds, we learned to abbreviate. I don't think anyone lost anything in the process."

"No, I don't think anyone lost anything!" Char's eyes were sparkling with the memories.

"Then they moved us from the southern end of Japan to this place called the Purple Farm, nearer the mountains. It was this old Japanese farmhouse with paper walls, and a cooking pit in the floor. They had a regular kitchen as well as the cooking pit. We were there a couple of days before we did any work. There was one guy who was very skeptical, and he spoke English very well, so he was able to verbalize his skepticism…"

Char cackled, "Very clearly!"

"…and he said 'Oh, this Shinto priest is coming and he is *much* more powerful than you!' It was a challenge."

"So I told him it would be a great honor."

"Yeah, Char handled it with great tact, she wasn't defeated by it, and she wasn't inflated by it. I was just sitting there thinking, well, this I gotta see, this I gotta see!" They both roared with laughter.

"So we had a couple of days to build the sweat and reflect, getting ready for this. I was very aware this guy was going to be in my sweat. We felt that we needed to be a little bit more at peace and not give too much away to him, not treat him any differently than anyone else. It's hard when you think someone really holy is going to be there, not to give it up and let them take over.

"So when he came, he was late, and we didn't meet him before the sweat, and I didn't know who he was, or even if he was there. The whole time the sweat was going on I was wondering if he was there, because I couldn't feel him. You know, the energy changes, when a powerful person is in the sweat you can tell. I could always feel Char or Mahdi when they came into the sweat. I can feel people, some are anxious, some are excited, some are totally bewildered and some are in a lot of pain. I was picking up all that but I wasn't picking up any Shinto priest! He had himself covered, that's the only explanation. In the end when he came out, we figured out who he was, everybody was talking to him and they were all over him. But he wouldn't talk to us, he wouldn't have anything to do with us. Later we went to dinner at the samurai's house—"

Char interjected quietly: "Oh, the samurai took my breath away!"

Carol laughed, saying, "Yes, he was a very cool guy! He lived just up the hill from where we were staying and when he heard we were there, he invited us over for dinner. It was one of those traditional Japanese houses, it was so cool, and the food was incredible!"

"Yes, but it was freezing once it got dark, it had no heating. They had to give us these big wool blankets."

"So who all went to dinner?" I asked, visualizing them sitting cross-legged on the floor around a low Japanese table. Carol flipped through the pile of photos, coming up with one that showed exactly this. She pointed everyone out.

"There we are: us, and Mahdi, and the Shinto priest, and the samurai and his family, and a couple of the people who had been at the retreat."

"So did the Shinto priest still ignore you?"

Carol laughed again, glancing at Char. "No, we had a couple of interesting interchanges with him, or rather, Char did!"

"I was interested in how someone becomes a Shinto priest, so I asked him what his training was, and he just kept saying that when he was a baby, he cried all the time, so they took him to the Shinto temple, and he stopped crying. I asked him twice, and that's all he would say." She raised her eyebrows, shrugging.

"Tell her about when he was saying he had cured someone!"

"Oh yes!" Char sat up, laughing. "When we were at dinner he kept hitting on this teenage kid who was there, she was some relative of the samurai's, and I could tell she wanted to get away from him, she didn't like the way he was touching her and talking to her, and nor did I! It was tacky. I hate it when people take advantage of their so-called spiritual position like that. Anyhow, at some point he was telling everyone how he had cured this woman with cancer, and he was boasting about how he could do healings, so I just said, 'I thought it was god who did the healing.'"

Carol rocked with delight at the memory. "She said it real quietly but everyone heard it, and the whole room went silent for a few seconds. It really put him in his place. He was so obnoxious!"

They showed me photos of the houses, the Shinto priest looking like all the other Japanese in the distance, and the samurai showing off his sword, which Char assured me is very rare.

Glancing at my watch, I realized it was already one, time for lunch. We went to a restaurant nearby, and I watched Char joking around with the waiter, making friends with the people at the next table. She ate her lunch slowly and delicately, exclaiming how delicious it was. When she was done, she left a small portion, which she put outside on the porch railing for spirit.

I bathed in her animated joyful warmth, wondering at my opportunity to write about this woman who is such a powerful wind of fresh air. What a gift, to be allowed to pry into the things she accepts as normal: the intimacy of her ongoing, ever-present relationship to spirit, how she works with energy, what she sees and how she interprets it. What a delight, to be able to ask all the questions I have ever wanted!

Part One

The Circumstances of Char's Childhood and Training

Chapter One

Matilda stood on the corner waiting for the phone, tapping her foot impatiently. She was small and young, and attractive enough to get second looks from some of the passersby: long jet black hair tied back, a heart shaped face, with evenly set features and dark eyes. At first glance, she appeared Caucasian, but it might occur to someone who thought about such things, that she had Native American or Hispanic blood. The fog was blowing in off the San Francisco Bay, carried on a wind that was chilly for late spring. She huddled in the Navy issue jacket with threaded gold anchors on the lapels, though it did nothing to protect her legs, exposed by the miniskirt that only came halfway down her thighs.

In 1967, being in the Navy was more for her than just an escape from a dysfunctional family, it was the source of her pride. She was one of the Blue Waves, the first women allowed into that prestigious institution. It was part of Matilda's ancestral lineage: her father, her grandfather, and her uncles, they had all been in the Navy.

The man who was using the phone slammed it down, walking off. She went to the booth. Tucking the phone into her shoulder, she fed coins in with one hand while holding her address book in the other. She waited, anxiously tapping her fingers on the phone rest. The phone rang twice, and a female voice picked up. "Jason Electronics, how may I help you?"

"I'd like to speak with Paul Wagner."

"Who's speaking, please?"

"Matilda."

"Please hold, I'll see if he's in."

She waited again, praying silently to some unknown god. This was the fifth time she had called him in a week, and the last four times she'd been told he was unavailable. The conversation they'd had when she told him her period was late ran in her head like a stuck tape: "I'm married," he'd said, his eyes suddenly cold, and his tone distant. "I already have two children, and I don't want any more. Besides, I don't have any reason to believe any baby of yours is mine." The unspoken accusation was still a knife in her belly.

In front of her, on the phone booth wall, an ad for vacuum cleaners showed a pretty young woman happily vacuuming a floor. She looked away.

The female voice returned. "I'm sorry, he's not in right now, would you like to leave a message?"

"Yes, please." She wanted to scream and hurl the phone at him. But he wasn't there, or he wasn't answering.

And he never would. This realization ran like a chilled fluid through the marrow of her bones. She dropped the phone, letting it dangle, twirling. For the first time, she allowed hot tears to leak out of her eyes, leaning her head against the wall of the booth as they ran down her cheeks.

The baby was due in six months. The Navy was her life, and now they would discharge her.

At three in the morning, the hospital was quiet, the delivery room empty but for her. Being a Navy hospital, they didn't have to deal with many babies.

"It'll be twelve hours at least before you are ready to give birth, I'm going to send you home." The unsmiling doctor still had pimples. He couldn't have been any older that she was.

"*Twelve hours*! I can't stand this for twelve hours! And I can't go home, my friends who brought me have left already!"

He was stripping off the latex gloves. "There's no point in you staying here overnight. You might as well go home and sleep."

She gripped the metal arms of the bed as another contraction grabbed her belly. He was the doctor, presumably he knew what he was talking about, but the idea of being home, dealing with this alone, filled her with dread. When she could catch her breath, she said, "I won't be able to sleep. I can't go home."

He had turned away, but now he turned back and glared down at her, deliberating. "Well, then, I suppose you can stay here. I'll give you something to make you sleep." He gave an order to the young white-hatted woman who stood beside him, and left without another glance. The nurse also disappeared, returning shortly with a syringe.

"Just a little prick," she said, as she inserted the needle.

"Is this going to dull the pain?" The question had a distinct tone of hopefulness.

"It might do...it will make you drowsy. You'll sleep through the pain."

She smiled reassuringly, and Matilda felt absurdly grateful.

The nurse left her in the sterile empty room, and she did fall into a fitful sleep, but the contractions grabbed her regularly every five minutes or so. She could not sleep through them. Strange dreams invaded her: that goofy commercial, the seven wonders of the cat world, and the Dodge Good Guys in their white hats. Soon the contractions were getting stronger and she began to sob. She didn't want to be alone with this alien force taking over her body. She pressed the bell for the nurse, and waited, trying to keep the fear at bay. The second the nurse entered, Matilda gasped, "I'm having this baby, I know it, get the doctor, please!"

The nurse looked anxious. "Well...no, the doctor says you're not ready yet."

"I am ready, I know I am!"

The white-hatted woman hovered by the bed. "You just need to relax and go to sleep."

"I can't! I'm ready to have the baby, I know it!"

The young nurse hesitated, uncertain. But her fear of the doctor won out, and all she did before she left was to adjust the bed so that Matilda wasn't lying quite so flat. "I'll check on you again shortly."

Another spasm twisted her belly. She lay there panting, sweat dripping down her sides and tears down her cheeks. Time passed. She dozed in between the contractions, hounded by the strange dreams of commercials. Another nurse came in, an older woman with a lined face and gray hair tied back in a bun. She had an air of efficiency and confidence. Hope flooding through her, Matilda gasped, "Oh, please, please get the doctor, I'm going to have the baby!"

The woman patted her arm and pulled on some gloves. "Well, I'll just take a quick look and see how dilated you are." Setting Matilda's feet in the stirrups, she pulled up the sheet. Her eyebrows raised. "My goodness, you are ready to have this baby!"

"I keep telling them that, they won't listen to me!"

"Well, the doctor should be here any minute."

"He won't come, I've been asking, and he won't come! He said it would be twelve hours before I was ready to have the baby!"

"Hmmm..." The nurse looked down at the distressed woman, assessing her pale face and black hair, damp with sweat, spread out on the white pillow. She pursed her lips.

She called the doctor from a phone in the corner of the room. Matilda almost laughed in spite of her anxiety and pain. Clearly, the nurse was of a higher rank than the doctor. Her tone brooked no opposition. "If you don't get down here right away, I will put you on report!"

He soon arrived, and the older woman departed. He busied himself filling out the paperwork while Matilda panted, thinking, *you jerk, you should have done that before.*

"Don't bear down now," he warned her as he scribbled.

"I'm trying not to!"

He glared at her again, snapping, "Well, then, don't!"

She turned her head away, letting the tears leak out onto the already damp pillow, as another contraction took over.

"Now, you're giving the baby up for adoption, is that correct?"

She caught her breath, as her muscles seized her and let go again. "Yes, it's all been arranged."

"Do you want to see the baby?"

"I can't!" *Don't they get it?*

More time passed and the young nurse was at her side. At last the doctor told her to bear down. She went into a state beyond the physical, where she didn't really feel the pain any more. Her body wasn't hers now. She gazed at the huge belly under the sheet, clenching and unclenching, as she floated over the bed waiting for it to be finished. Finally the baby moved down, splitting open the body it was leaving. There was some hustle and bustle.

"Is it a boy or a girl?" she asked, her voice hoarse.

"A healthy little girl," replied the nurse with a smile. "Do you want to see her?"

"No!" Matilda was adamant. As she closed her eyes, she caught sight of the clock on the wall; it was eight o'clock in the morning.

The nurse carried the infant out of the room.

She sat at the table, staring blankly out of the window at the rain that fell in steady spears. A paper sat in front of her, waiting for her signature, but the pen beside it lay unheeded, while a cigarette smoked itself slowly to death in the ashtray. She sat there for a long time, just as she had been sitting for most of the past seven days.

At last she reached out and picked up the phone, cupping her still aching breast with the other hand. She read a number off the paper, and dialed it.

"Hallo, is this Mrs. Jackson? This is Matilda Goodrich…yes, the little girl…a week ago…no, I've changed my mind, I want to keep her."

The ride to the foster home was briefer than she expected. The house was pale blue, set back off the street, with a garden that was probably beautiful in the spring. Matilda didn't even see the garden. Mrs. Jackson walked up the path with her, and rang the doorbell. As they waited, she turned to Matilda. "Now you're quite sure this is what you want?"

Matilda nodded, gazing at her blankly, and Mrs. Jackson put a consoling hand on her arm, saying, "It's all right, dear, I know you've been thinking about this very hard."

The door opened and a handsome man in his early thirties, with cropped reddish hair, motioned them in without saying a word.

"Janice, they're here!" he called, and they followed him into a tastefully furnished living room, with muted colors. There were signs that children had been here: the top half of a one armed doll stuck out from under the corner of the sofa, a child's cup sat on the table. The man turned to the visitors. "She'll be here in a moment. Perhaps you would like to sit down," he motioned to the chairs. Mrs. Jackson sat down, but Matilda remained standing, staring awkwardly around, seeing nothing.

A woman with tightly curled blonde hair came in, carrying a bundle wrapped in a blue shawl. Her eyes, though round and kind, were puffy, the look of recent tears reddening around them. She went straight to Matilda, and the muscles of her face composed themselves into something resembling a smile, her lips remaining tightly lined. "You must be this little one's mother."

The baby stared up at Matilda. What did those unwavering blue eyes see? One tiny hand was free of the shawl and Matilda put her finger in it, as though to shake hands. The baby clenched her fingers around it, and gurgled.

The woman who was holding her said, "She's a wonderful baby. I've held her a lot, so she's had plenty of affection."

"She's beautiful!" They were the first words Matilda had uttered for at least an hour. She took the baby into her arms. "I'm going to call her Charlotte, after my mother!"

The blonde woman stood holding her empty hands in front of her heart, as tears filled her eyes. Matilda turned towards the door.

The baby was lying in her crib, staring up at the mobile made of shiny stars that twirled gently in the warm Hawaiian breeze. She gurgled and cooed, and reached up with her little hands, exploring her naked toes as her legs waved in the air. Her grandfather folded his newspaper, leaning back in his rocking chair with a sigh. He stared out at the palm trees that lined the street in front of the verandah, but he wasn't seeing them; he was listening to the sounds the baby was making. After a while he got up and went to the crib. He smiled down at the child, touching her cheek gently with his big calloused fingers. They laughed at each other. "Little moanie groanie, that's what you are," he said.

Matilda came up behind him, and hearing what he said, she laughed too. "She does make a lot of funny noises, doesn't she?"

"Yes, she's a little moanie groanie!"

"Come on, you little moanie groanie, it's time you got fed." She picked the baby up, cradling her little blonde head in her hand. They sat down on the settee, while the baby sucked greedily on the bottle. The man took one of the chairs and turned it around, sitting astride it with his arms across the back of the chair, so that he faced them. He was silent for a while but he was no longer smiling, and the air was laden with unsaid words.

Finally he spoke. "Matilda, what are you going to do?"

She didn't look at him, idly stroking the baby's blonde hair and staring into her crystal blue eyes. After a little pause, she said, with a stubborn tone, "We've been over this before, Dad, I'll get a job and find somewhere to live on my own."

"You're not addressing the problem, you know that. You need a man to take care of you and the baby."

There was a long silence. The only movement in the room was the slight twirling of the mobile in the breeze, and the child vigorously sucking at the warm formula.

He spoke again, and this time the anger in his voice was unveiled. "Dammit, Matilda, can't you see we are just worried for you? Why don't you come to your senses and marry Dwayne? He wants to marry you!"

She turned a stubborn frown on her father, "Because I don't love him."

"For god's sake, Matilda, you can learn to love him! He's a good man, he'll take care of you!"

In a flash of fury, Matilda stood up, the baby in her arms, the baby bottle falling to the floor. "Very well then, dammit, I will marry him, since it seems to be the only thing that makes you happy!" She spat the words, storming out of the room. The baby's little face crinkled and she set up a wail that stayed in the man's ears long after they were out of earshot.

Dwayne was still in the Navy, and shortly after their son, Stewart, was born, he was stationed in Hawaii. Matilda had mixed feelings about being there. On the one hand she liked the weather and the surroundings, and being near her parents was a plus, as they were helpful with the children. On the other hand, she had no friends here, and there was very little nightlife, so she was lonely. Dwayne was away on duty most of the time. Because they were married with kids, they couldn't live on the base, and she had an apartment in town.

That evening Mike and Bill were coming over. She didn't know them well, but they were friends of Dwayne's from the service and he had asked them to visit, since he knew she was lonely. She glanced at the clock; they would be here soon. She went in to the kids' room. The baby, Stewart, was asleep, snuggled into orange sheets, and Charlotte was sitting in the middle of the room in her pajamas. She was crooning to herself, and seemed absorbed in the white wall in front of her. As Matilda came in, she looked up, her eyes aquamarine in the evening light, and said, "Look, Mommy, look how pretty they are!" She pointed at the wall.

Her mother bent down to pick her up. "I don't see anything, sweetheart, but if you think it's pretty, that's good. It's time for bed now, are you going to lie down, and be a good girl? I'll read to you."

She read from *Charlotte's Web*, and the little girl fell asleep with her blonde hair over her face. Matilda walked back along the hallway, switching on the light. The gecko that shared the apartment, paying its rent by eating insects, scuttled along the wall beside her. She greeted it with a smile. "Hello, little fella, how are you this evening?"

The gecko clicked in response, then ran back up to the ceiling as the doorbell sounded. Matilda let the men in. They sat down to eat the pizza that they had brought, exclaiming how they missed the pizza parlors from back home. Afterwards, she produced cold beers from the refrigerator, and they sat around joking, talking of nothing. The conversation lulled, and Mike asked her if she played poker.

She shook her head. "No, I've never been any good at cards. I tell you what, though, I've got a ouija board in the closet over there, we could play with that if you like! I've never actually played with one but I've heard of people getting interesting stuff."

"Bit different from poker!" said Mike, laughing. "Sure, let's give it a whirl. I've never used one before, I don't even know how you do it."

"I used one with some friends when we were kids," said Bill. "We got some words but I think it was one of my friends fooling around."

They set the board on the table, pulling their chairs up so they could all reach it.

"So how do you start?"

"We all just put our fingers on the pointer—" she indicated the board "—and concentrate, until it moves of its own accord, and points to a letter."

"Don't put too much pressure on the pointer, or you will stop it moving," added Bill.

They sat in silence, without any change in the position of the pointer. Mike laughed. "How long do we have to sit here before it moves?"

"Let's try it a little longer, sometimes it takes a while," said Bill. Just then the pointer jerked to one side and then the other.

"Whoa!" exclaimed Mike in surprise. "Which one of you is making it do that?"

"Neither of us, that's the spirits!" replied Matilda, excited.

"You mean ghosts? I'm not so sure about this!" The pointer took off down the board, moving rapidly, and Mike jerked his hand back in surprise. "Hey, what's going on, that felt weird!"

"My god, look at the curtains!" Bill was facing the window, his eyes huge. The other two followed his gaze. The curtains were standing straight out, parallel to the floor.

Mike jumped up. "Fuck it, man, what's going on? That's not funny!" He glanced wildly around the room.

Bill stood up, a little calmer but still obviously shaken. "That's not the wind doing that, is it? Christ, there *isn't* any fucking wind!"

"The window's closed," said Matilda, calmly.

"Hey man, I'm going home, this isn't funny!" Mike grabbed his jacket, backing towards the door before he remembered his manners. Turning to Matilda, he said, "Uh…I hope you don't mind, I just don't like this kind of stuff. Thanks for having us over."

"It's nothing to worry about, you know. Whatever is doing that, it's not malevolent."

"Sure, well…we'll be seeing you!"

Matilda locked the door behind them. When she turned back, the curtains were hanging normally. Shrugging, she went into the back room and checked on the children. Charlotte had pushed the cover off but she was still sleeping soundly. Stewart was just waking up. She carried him into the living room to feed him.

After a year in Hawaii, they were sent to the Philippines. A ten foot chain link fence surrounded the compound where they had a house, and outside that fence was the jungle, impenetrable and mysterious. Local Filipinos, paid by the US government, patrolled between the fence and the jungle to make sure the white Americans were not troubled by hidden horrors that might creep in from that strange untamed place.

Matilda took the children to the playground in the compound, Stewart in the stroller, while Char skipped alongside. For her third birthday her grandparents had given her a doll in a flowery dress, with blue eyes that blinked. Today she brought the doll along, dragging it by one arm as she held onto the stroller, singing to herself in a mixture of Tagalog (the native language) and English.

At the playground, Char put Stewart, still barely able to walk, on the swing, and pushed him, while Matilda chatted to the other bored mothers sitting on the benches in the shade, complaining about the heat. Tired of the swings, Char put Stewart on the merry-go-round, and with the help of some older children, pushed it as fast as she could. Matilda, seeing this, came over and was about to intervene, when Stewart let go. He landed on his butt and rolled over. Matilda ran to him but he pushed himself upright, undeterred, and when she fussed over him, he ignored her, intent on returning to the merry-go-round, wanting to feel the exhilaration of the wind in his little face again. Matilda shrugged, going back to the bench.

"He's such a tough little thing," she remarked to one of the other mothers.

"Sure is," she agreed, dryly. "If that had been my Johnny, he'd have been screaming."

Done with the merry-go-round, Char returned to the swings. Stewart wandered over to his mother, asking for a drink. His home sewn pants and shirt, carefully made by Matilda to match Char's, were scuffed and dirty. She put him in the stroller. "It's time for lunch." She raised her voice, calling, "Come on, Charlotte, we're going home!"

"I'm coming!" the little girl replied. She picked up the doll, that was lying face down in the dirt, and placed it on the swing, giving it one little push before she ran to join her mom.

Matilda, intent on buckling Stewart into the stroller, didn't see this, but as they were going in the front door of their house, she noticed that the doll was missing.

"Charlotte, what happened to that doll?"

"At the playground!" Char skipped off down the passageway.

"Charlotte, that's the third time you've left your dolls at the playground! I'm not going to buy you any more, you know! We don't have enough money for you to be throwing them away!"

The little girl didn't seem at all perturbed at her mother's annoyance. She was running off to find the maid. Matilda took the sleeping Stewart to put him in his cot. When she came back, she glanced in the kitchen door. Char was sitting at the kitchen table, listening with rapt attention to the maid, who was talking to her in Tagalog, of which Matilda understood not a word. She shrugged, leaving them to it.

Later that day, when the maid had departed, Char was playing with her crayons on the porch, experimenting with all her different colors, drawing unidentifiable pictures as she hummed to herself. After she had filled several sheets of paper, she got up and went to the porch railing, looking over at the chain link fence, twenty yards away. There were the children dressed only in loin cloths, running in and out of the forest, their brown bodies alternately dappled with sun and shade. Some wore beautifully crafted headdresses of macaw feathers. Char trotted down the steps off the porch and over to the fence, entwining her fingers in the links. Two of the children came over to greet her. They laughed with pleasure at seeing her, putting their brown fingers next to hers in the fence. "Come and play with us!" grinned the bigger of the two.

"How can I get over?"

He indicated a culvert, a little to their left. "You could get through here!" He knelt down at one end with his sister, and the two of them called into the metal pipe, the echo of their voices making eerie sounds. Char knelt down at her end, and sure enough, she found she could crawl through. She was delighted.

Matilda was feeding Stewart when she realized that she hadn't heard from Char for a while. She called, and hearing no answer, went out to look. The porch was empty except for crayons and paper scattered about. The yard gate stood open, but that was normal. She glanced around, at the fence, at the houses and yards to either side. There was no sign of anyone. She felt a fleeting surge of panic, and then it was gone, as though someone had said, "Don't worry, we're taking care of her, she's fine."

She stood on the porch for a minute, assessing her options, then walked along the road calling Char. She still wasn't worried, though she kept thinking she should be. At the end of the road, she started back.

She was halfway to the house when she saw Char happily skipping towards her, holding the hand of one of the Filipino guards. The two of them looked incongruous, he with his brown body in shorts and shirt, dark hair and eyes, she with her blonde hair, white skin—tanned but far from dark—and brilliant blue eyes. "Mommy!" she called.

Matilda replied, "Charlotte, baby, where have you been?"

"Playing with my friends!" Char smiled up at her mother ingenuously. Matilda was puzzled; to her knowledge, the child had no friends who lived close by.

The dark-skinned man spoke. "I found her on the other side of the fence, Ma'am!" Unlike Char and Matilda, he was visibly anxious. "I think she's OK."

"Was she with any other kids?"

He shook his head. "No, she was alone."

"How did she get out?"

"I think she must have crawled through one of the culverts."

"Well, thank you very much for bringing her back!" She took Char's hand.

"I'll make sure the culvert is blocked off." The man looked down at the little girl affectionately. "I hope she is OK!"

"She looks fine to me!"

He nodded, smiled goodbye, and went off down the street. As they walked back to the house, Matilda said, "Charlotte, you mustn't go on the other side of the fence, it's dangerous."

The little girl glanced up at her mother with a look that was almost quizzical, saying, "My friends take care of me, and they have beautiful things!"

Chapter Two

The marriage with Dwayne lasted three years before Matilda moved, with the children, to Bremerton, just south of Seattle, to live on welfare. She fell into the state of depression that hounded her whenever she was without a partner. Nearly three hard years passed. Char was seven when her mother finally met Keith at Twelve Step Meetings, and they moved across the mountains together, to a small farm house in the wheat fields near Colfax. Matilda was happy there, gardening, canning, cooking, and sewing all day. Although they often had chores to do on the little farm, the two children deeply appreciated the freedom of living in the country. Delighted with any opportunity to learn about Nature, Char loved all the life around them, including the insects, the cats and the ever present dog, Sunshine.

Char, Stewart and Matilda were all a little afraid of Keith. He liked to rule the roost and was quite ready to beat the children when they did something he considered out of order. His temper was not always predictable. But in those days, before he started drinking again, he was frequently affectionate and entertaining. He taught the children how to use guns, and took them hunting. They didn't have TV, so on the long winter evenings, Matilda sewed, while Keith sat in the big armchair reading, with a child on either side, glued to the sound of his voice. They read the classics, such as *The Little House on the Prairie*, *Charlotte's Web*, *Stuart Little*, and *The Lord of the Rings*. The children were always entranced, demanding that Keith carry on long after he was exhausted, eager to know what would happen next. They discussed the characters at length, speculating on their qualities, and wondering how it would turn out in the end.

School time came. In the mornings, Matilda stood with her children at the end of the short driveway that led to their house, waiting for the yellow bus, listening to the occasional meadowlark singing its beautiful melody. Char enjoyed these early mornings. She would squint at the sun as it crept slowly up the sky, experimenting with the colors she then saw when she looked at other things. Noticing this, Matilda told her off. "Stop looking at the sun, Charlotte, if you're not careful you'll go blind!"

Char turned this idea over in her mind. Young though she was, she had read all of Helen Keller's books (arguing with the surprised and slightly disapproving librarian about whether she was old enough to appreciate them), and she revered the blind woman as an idol. So the idea of being blind herself was not at all frightening to her; in fact it was quite interesting. She continued to look at the sun, finding great joy in the colors and beauty it created. She felt one with the sun when she looked at it, as though her body didn't exist in the material world. When she looked away, everything was changed, covered in spots, and she would see greens, blues, oranges, reds or yellows where there had been no particular color before. She began to experiment with being blind; she would close her eyes as she got onto the school bus, feeling her way, and she often didn't open them again until she was in the school yard. She didn't mind that the other kids thought she was strange; she experienced herself as different from them, anyway, and that belief was fostered by Matilda, who constantly told her she was special.

One night, Char was dreaming about being carried by an undertow of blue warmth, surrounded by a white wave. The need to pee woke her. She opened her eyes and pulled the bedclothes back, swinging her short legs onto the soft blue carpet at the edge of the bed. She padded towards the door, careful not to slip as the carpet turned to wood. It was some indefinable time in the night, and the house was silent, still and dark, but it was not the kind of impenetrable darkness that prevented her from making out the shapes of the furniture. She stepped into the living room. A figure stood about ten feet away from her: a woman in long robes, swirling with color. The form was glowing with light that laced through it, pulsating and flowing as she stood there smiling at the child. Through the being's transparent body, Char could make out the fireplace behind her.

Char stared, entranced. Something about this presence was vitally important. She felt like she was standing in warm sunlight, her body bathed and soothed by the rays. A physical sensation of love filled her up, as though she were standing under a shower and her body was permeable to the delightful feeling of the water flowing over and through her. There was a complete absence of fear, a sense of total peace. In that long timeless moment, which might have been five minutes and might have been half an hour, Char knew that she was protected and guided, knew that she could always trust in the infinite compassion of the spirit world. She felt, rather than heard, the words that were spoken: "This kind of peace, this knowing of perfection, is always yours. You will always be safe, little one...we will always be here for you, and you will find that pain is always followed by joy. Everything is worth it, there is always love."

The being gradually faded, and Char continued along the hallway to pee. When she came back, the space in front of the fireplace was empty. She could still feel the loving presence.

In the morning, she went down to breakfast, which she always enjoyed. Matilda had made porridge, dotted with fat swollen raisins, and her steaming bowl sat waiting at the table. With the careful concentration that Char applied to everything she did, she made a dip in the middle and put a pat of butter in the hole, watching it melt to golden liquid. She sprinkled brown sugar liberally over the top, then poured on a little milk so that it pooled around the edge. She waited a moment or two, making sure it was cool enough to eat, and then took a carefully measured spoonful from the bottom of the bowl, including a little of everything: porridge, raisins, butter, sugar, and milk. Suddenly her preoccupation dropped away, as she remembered the figure she had seen the night before. She turned excitedly to Matilda. "Mommy, I saw someone standing in front of the fireplace last night! She was wearing a long dress, and you could see right through her!" Her blue eyes were wide.

Matilda ate a mouthful of her own porridge. "Well, did she frighten you?"

"No, she was beautiful!" Char laughed at the delight of the memory.

Her mother smiled. "Well, that's great! You saw your first ghost!"

The Palouse River was about a quarter of a mile down the hill from the house. A meadow of camass grew between the river and the farm. When it was in flower, it was vivid in its blue-ness, and rich with the smell that wafted on the breeze. One morning in late spring, Matilda quietly woke Char while it was still dark, whispering to her to get dressed. They crept out the door together, hand in hand, and walked through the growing light to the field that was full of the gorgeous blue camass, which had just come into bloom. They followed the gentle slope, both of them drawing deep breaths of the early morning scent, filling their nostrils with the astonishing fragrance. The orange and purple of sunrise streaked the sky as the light grew, until the red ball of the sun lifted itself over the edge of the earth. It was an extraordinary dawn, radiating beauty beyond imagination, filled with a scent that was heavenly.

When they got to the river, the water giving off the faintest bluish tinge from the snow melt higher up, Matilda told her about the people who had lived here long ago. "The native people would dig up the roots of the camass and they would dry them and grind them here. You see this stone with a hollow in it?" She pointed out the waist high rock that stood out from the other boulders piled at random along the course of the river. They both leaned against its cold surface, looking into the stone's bowl. "These are the stones they used for grinding. The people who live in the big house by the road remember the Nez Perce riding down to the river years ago in the spring to dig and grind the camass roots."

"Why don't *we* do that?" asked the little blonde girl, tracing the smooth perimeter of the stone with one finger.

Matilda laughed. "Well, I suppose we could! But it would be a lot of work and we have enough food."

"Who are the Nez Perce?"

"They are one of the native tribes who lived on this land." Matilda took Char's hand again, and they found a spot to sit where they were surrounded by the blue flowers, but still could watch the fast flowing river. In some places the water rushed by, creating flashes of foam in between rocks; in others, it slowed down to form deep, quietly circling eddies.

"Do the Nez Perce still live here?" Char was not finished with this conversation.

"The white people rounded most of them up and made them live in reservations. Many of them have died, because the reservations are often difficult places to live and when the white people invaded America, they took over all the native people's lands. They destroyed their way of life. They didn't like the native people, they killed lots of them. There were many battles. The native people knew how to live without hurting the land, and the white people don't know how to do that. They don't know that the rocks are alive and that plants have feelings."

"Do they pick the first flowers?" Matilda had always taught her kids that you never pick the first flower that appears.

"Yes…they don't respect the Earth. They don't realize it's sacred. They don't know about herbs and healing, they don't honor the cycles of life. Your dad's mother was Cheyenne, he knows lots of stuff. My mom was part Apache, but she won't talk about it much. So you're part Native American."

"Why won't she talk about it?"

"Lots of white people are ashamed of their Indian blood. They don't realize how wise the native people are."

"That's silly."

Matilda looked down affectionately and hugged the child to her. "You're right, it is silly."

They sat there for a few minutes in silence, admiring the beauty around them, and a butterfly flitted over them, its brown wings flashing with yellow as they caught the sun.

"A butterfly!" exclaimed Char, with a smile.

"Yes, do you remember that song we made up the other day when we were sitting outside the house, and those butterflies kept coming to visit us?"

"Yes!" They started singing in unison, the rushing of the river forming a backdrop to the beauty of their lilting voices.

A few days later, out at the barn, Keith addressed the children as he lifted his rod down off its hooks. "Come on, we're going fishing this morning. The water'll be high with the rain, and the trout will be feeding."

"Oh, goodie, goodie!' said Stu and Char in unison. They were just finishing up feeding the animals, which was one of their daily chores. They each picked up one side of a bucket filled with grain, and carried it out to the calf's feed trough.

A short while later, all four of them, accompanied by Sunshine, made their way down to a deep pool in the river. Keith was carrying his rod, and five year old Stu proudly held a can for the grasshoppers they used as bait. The fast flowing water was slightly muddy. The fish were jumping, just as Keith had said. He showed them how to thread a grasshopper on the hook, then he flung the line far out into the stream, at the top of the pool. Char and Matilda sat on a rock nearby.

"This rain we've been having is good for the land, it'll make things grow," said Matilda.

"Plants like the rain?"

"Yes, they need plenty of water. That's what makes them green. That's why everything gets brown in the summer, because it's so dry."

"And the fish like the rain too?"

"Yes, it brings down lots of food for them."

"They eat other things as well as grasshoppers?" The little girl leaned against Matilda's side, stroking the woman's long black hair with one hand, as she looked up earnestly with her bright aquamarine eyes.

"They eat worms and all kinds of insects, all sorts of little creepy crawleys. When they're jumping, they're eating flies that are buzzing around just above the water."

Char pursed her lips as she considered this. "But the *animals* don't like the rain, they have nowhere dry to go!"

"Well, they find dry places under trees and rocks, and besides, most of them have long coats. They don't mind the rain because they don't feel the cold like us, and they know that the rain brings growth."

"But insects don't have long coats! What happens to the ants that have nests in the ground? They must get flooded!"

"Well…" Matilda was searching for an answer to this when she noticed Keith. "Look, your dad has caught a fish!" They both ran down to the water's edge, where Keith, with a grin, was playing a sizeable trout into the shallows. Stu was jumping up and down beside him with little yelps of excitement. As Char and Matilda arrived, Keith grabbed hold of the fish, and took a handy rock to give it a sharp blow on the head, which stilled some of its frantic flipping. He gave it to Matilda, who used her sharp pocket knife to cut a slit up its belly. She emptied the intestines out onto the ground. Char examined the little pile with curiosity.

"Look, Mom, what's this orange stuff?"

"I think that's the roe. That's what they make babies with."

"Does that mean it was a girl fish?"

Matilda wasn't too sure of the reproductive mechanism of fish. "Ummm… I think it means it was a boy. Come on, we should go and wash this further down the river." She stood up, but Char was using a stick to poke through the small pile of guts on the ground.

"Mom, where's its heart? Fish have hearts, don't they?"

"All animals have hearts." Matilda bent down beside her and they finally came up with a little red triangular thing that seemed like it must be the heart. Satisfied, they went to wash the fish in the water. Later, Char had her turn with the rod, and caught two small ones in quick succession. Keith shook his head, laughing, and tousled her hair as she pulled the second one out. "You sure do have a knack for this, little girl!"

The next day, they went down to the river again and hunted for crawdads, which was one of Char's favorite things to do. She was very good at it, with her keen eyes and quick fingers, and her complete lack of fear of being bitten. They waded in the cold running water, often over their knees, picking up rocks close to shore. Whenever they saw a crawdad skittering away from under the rock, they grabbed it behind its little pinchers, quick as a flash, and put it in the coffee can that Matilda held. When they had a number of them, they made a fire right there by the water, and cooked them in the can. The moist tasty flesh melting in her mouth was a joy that Char never forgot.

On the way home, Matilda pointed out the elderflower bush that grew by the river, covered now in fragrant white flowers. "Look, you can eat these flowers, they're very tasty. And they are good for you, elderflower is a good tonic. You can make tea with them."

"Shall we pick some to take home now?" asked Char.

"No," said Matilda, "they'll make delicious berries in the summer, and we'll come pick those instead. Let's leave the flowers."

"Are the berries like rosehips?" asked Char, recalling a previous lesson from the year before.

Matilda smiled with pleasure at her daughter's good memory. "No, they are different, darker and smaller, and they grow in clumps. But it's good that you remember the rosehips! Do you remember what they are good for?"

Char grinned and skipped. "They're good for your blood, they're full of Vitamin C, and you can make tea with them!"

Matilda laughed, putting her arm affectionately around her daughter's shoulders. "Charlotte, you are so smart! You are really so special!"

The animals they kept on the farm were a constant source of entertainment. Matilda and the two children went out every day to feed the sheep, giving them left over scraps from the table, or other tidbits. One day they had a bag of prunes. Stewart dug his hand into the bag, looking at the wrinkled brown nubs. "You *made* these, Mom?" He sounded disgusted.

She clicked her tongue at him in annoyance. "Yes, Stewart, they are the plums that you helped pick off the plum trees just down there." She nodded towards the thicket down below the yard, by the ruined homestead.

"Why do they look like this?"

"Because they're dried! And you love them when I soak them and make your morning cereal with them, so don't turn your nose up at them now! Look, Clementine loves them too!"

The two sheep were waiting for their treats. Both the kids climbed up on the wooden fence to get a better view. Matilda offered Clementine one of the prunes and the woolly white animal ate it greedily, chewing in a sideways motion, and spitting the pit out so that it hit the fence with a ping. Matilda laughed. "You kids had better be careful, that pit'll hurt if it hits you! I don't know how she does it, but she spits them out with some force!"

"Mom, give me one for Mister, he's hungry!" Char put out her hand, and Matilda gave her a prune.

"You can try, but he doesn't like them."

Char fed him one off the palm of her hand and sure enough, although he took it in his black lips, he immediately dropped it on the muddy ground inside their pen.

"Doesn't matter, Clementine will come and eat it," said Stewart, watching the drama with interest from his vantage point atop the fence.

Matilda laughed again. "No, she won't, she doesn't like them when they are dirty!"

"That's not fair!" Char sounded quite upset, so Matilda gave her several more to feed to Clementine, which she did, enjoying the sheep's obvious appreciation. But Mister was clearly put out; he pushed his way in, knocking the prunes out of the girl's hand. So they went on to look at the chickens instead, two hundred of them parading around the barn and the fenced area outside.

"Your dad says I have to slaughter them soon," said Matilda, with a sigh.

"How are you going to do that?" asked Char, doubtfully.

"I suppose I'll cut their heads off. Then we'll have to pluck and clean them."

"We have to kill all two hundred of them?" Char looked a little appalled. "What will we do without their eggs?" She loved the daily ritual of feeding the chickens and going through the henhouse to search the straw laden boxes for warm oval treasures.

"He says we have to kill Mister and Clementine too," piped up Stewart.

"Yes, I know he says that! I want to keep them, they make such good lawnmowers," said Matilda, sighing again.

"But they are farm animals, right?" said Char, repeating what she had heard her father say. "We bought them for meat, didn't we?"

"Yes," said Matilda, fretfully, "But I don't want to kill them! They're our friends!"

In the end, Matilda did kill the chickens by cutting their heads off, forcing herself to do twenty a day for ten days. She hated it, and told Stewart to pray that none of them would suffer, so he stood by saying, "Please god, don't let any of the chickens get hurt!" while she did the dirty deed.

Neither Stewart nor Char were present when the sheep were killed, but they both helped for long hours with the chickens, dunking the limp bodies in hot water prior to plucking. Char had a clear understanding that the end of the physical form was not the end of life, and that everything that lives also dies. She was used to blood and gore, since her dad had been hunting ever since they'd moved out here, often coming home with deer or rabbits that needed to be skinned and cleaned. So when the calf was slaughtered, she came to watch, quite intrigued. Tying the animal up outside the barn, Keith shot him in the head, then hauled the body up by its hind legs, so that it hung upside down just off the ground. He took his knife, making a slit from tail to sternum, careful not to cut too deep. The two pieces of flesh split open, revealing the neatly folded guts within. The tall man smiled down at Char's curious face as she stood beside him, and said, "Do you want to pull the guts out?"

The girl looked up at him. "What do I have to do?"

"Just reach your hands behind the guts as far as you can, up by the tail, and pull downwards."

She stepped forward and stood on tiptoe, sliding her hands inside the slit as he had instructed, feeling the backbone hard against the backs of her hands. The calf's warm soft flesh felt good to her. Threading her fingers into the pink warmth, she pulled down. The guts came cascading outwards into a steaming red pile at her feet, and Keith stepped forward to help pull away the pieces that remained attached to the carcass.

One day, Char was shopping in Colfax with her mother. As she walked along, trailing a little behind, she noticed that there was something different about Matilda. She watched curiously. She couldn't put a name to what was going on, but she knew that Matilda was walking differently, and for no apparent reason, she knew that it was something really wonderful.

So she figured out before anyone else did, that Matilda was pregnant. It was very unexpected, since Keith had been exposed to Agent Orange in Vietnam, and the doctors had told him he was sterile. When Conrad was born, he doted on him, and so did Char. But Matilda insisted that they move to Wenatchee, because she knew she wouldn't be able to do all the work on the farm, as well as take care of a baby. When Conrad was one month old, they said goodbye to the old house in the wheat fields that had been so good to them, and went back to the town.

Chapter Three

Later, Char referred to that time on the farm as the happiest years of her life. Things quickly changed once they were in town. Keith soon found himself another woman, and the family dissolved. For a while Char saw him regularly, then he faded out of her life. Matilda and the kids moved every few months, always short on cash.

Unlike most children, Char did not lose her ability to see in other realms as she grew older; at one of the houses where they lived, she played with a ghost who inhabited the attic. She and her brother Stewart grew accustomed to developing their own resources as Matilda sank deeper and deeper into a morass of depression. The times when she surfaced grew horribly brief. Rage seemed to be her only motivation, the only feeling that could catalyze her into activity. She saw a psychiatrist, though her daughter never heard any diagnosis beyond her own and Stewart's: "Mom's fallen down and can't get up." Barely able to keep herself alive, Matilda certainly couldn't deal with the demands of a toddler and two precocious children.

Stewart, always uncontrollable, was the first to be sent away. Matilda tolerated her daughter much longer, since Char had such a sweet nature, and adored Conrad, taking care of him very capably. But as she entered her teens, Char wanted to go out more and more with her friends. She didn't take well to the restrictions that her mother tried to place on her. They were constantly at loggerheads. Finally Matilda reached her limit, and it was Char's turn to leave. Her pleas were met with angry justifications. "I need time to breathe myself back to life, you'll only be away for three months," Matilda said, as she turned away, retreating into blankness.

The drive to the foster home in Chelan passed in silence, broken only by the sobs that Char tried to contain. When they said goodbye, Matilda was careful not to meet her daughter's tear-filled eyes.

Three months stretched to one year, and then to two.

Despite this rejection, Char embraced everything around her with such uninhibited warmth that most people could not help loving her, and her new family was no different. She enjoyed the excitement of running away occasionally with the other foster child, a gay boy, but she didn't object when the police returned them. Although she was infuriated when her Christian foster parents burned her record collection, "to save her from the clutches of Satan," she was very curious about the Four Square Church. A natural singer, she loved to join in the choir, and found the youth group intriguing. Once, she even spoke in tongues, which she later realized was about channeling an entity, or entities. When she agreed to be baptized into the church, thinking it might be an experience worth having, she was deeply inspired by the priest in charge of the ceremony. Seeing him surrounded with flowing light, she perceived that he was blessed in some very wonderful way. She conceived an ambition that never left her: she wanted to be like him, a healer blessed by spirit. She wanted to lead a life that would be in service to god, she just wasn't quite sure *which* god. One thing she did know—it wouldn't be a god who disapproved of the music she loved.

When Char was fourteen, Keith turned up out of nowhere. It was about three years since she'd last seen him. The brevity of his words, "I'm here to get you," was typical, and she didn't trust them. He had failed her before, why would he not do so again? Still, her heart lifted when she saw his tall lean form standing in the doorway of the big house that had become her home. He was family, and he wanted her.

Keith's striking blue eyes, inherited from his white father, were much like Char's, inherited from *her* white father, who disowned her before she was born. He had a certain charisma, enhanced by some shamanic training, which usually got him what he wanted. They went to the two bedroom house he rented in Wenatchee, where he lived with his girlfriend, Laura, only four years Char's senior. He informed Char that he was ready to initiate her in the ways of a traditional medicine woman, as soon as she agreed. Char was interested, but unsure: was this going to help her in connecting to the flowing light she'd seen around the priest? By this time, she was accustomed to forming her own opinions, making her own judgments about what she considered right, or useful. Keith made it clear that if she agreed to an apprenticeship with him, she would not have the option of saying no. She would not be allowed to exercise her own judgment—at least, not to him.

He displayed his psychic talents, sitting opposite Char while she thoroughly shuffled a deck of cards. Holding them under the table where he could not see them, she pulled one card at a time. Keith named each one, making only a couple of mistakes in the entire deck. Char was impressed. Though still uncertain that this training would connect her with spirit in the way she wanted, Char knew of no other path. She agreed to the apprenticeship.

Her first experience of the many rituals they did together was a naming ceremony at the kitchen table. Emptying a ziplock bag full of rocks, Keith arranged them carefully in a circle, as his eerie chanting filled the air, and the smoke of incense spiraled through the room, blue in the flickering candlelight. Then he drummed, pausing only to mix some clay with water in a bowl, and paint Char's face with his fingers. "Little Fawn" was the name he gave her, telling her he would teach her how to move through the world with the silent grace and vision of a deer. Secretly, she resented the cloying sweetness of the name; she wanted to be fiercely powerful, like a cougar. But she was careful how she articulated any dissatisfaction. Many things that rankled went unquestioned.

Keith took her out of school so she could focus on her spiritual training. She didn't mind missing school, since she thought schoolwork was silly, and the teachers tended to think of her as a bad influence: she was too uninhibited, too much at ease with herself, too entranced by life and all its different opportunities.

Now her stepfather dictated her reality, keeping the door of the house locked so she could not leave without his permission. The only other people she saw regularly were Laura (his girlfriend), and Annie, a friend of Char's from the days of school. Annie and Laura were under Keith's thrall as much as she, though her friendship with Annie was a bedrock that helped to anchor her. The two of them spent days sewing patches on jeans and jackets in Char's room, listening to music. In the summer, Keith took them on trips to canyons and forests to teach them about the power and beauty of Nature.

For a few months, her brother Stewart came to live with them, also as an apprentice. One day, Keith discovered that Stewart had been shoplifting. In front of Char, he beat him with his bare fists, until the boy stopped trying to get up off the floor. Then he loaded him into the car and took him back to a foster home. Char didn't see her brother again for several years.

After a while, Char lost her ability to tell, from moment to moment, whether she was operating in a physical or a shamanic realm of consciousness. Strange things frequently happened, such as the jackets hanging on the door flying abruptly across the room. No one questioned such occurrences. The days were full of riddles, stories and tests. Keith ignored her half the time, and the other half, he focused on her so intensely she had no space to think her own thoughts. Teaching in the traditional manner, he rarely answered her questions directly. He never acknowledged her skills, and even when he was being affectionate, he called her "shithead." Sometimes he woke her before dawn, ordering her to sit outside, half naked, to greet the sun. She learned the joy of stillness, along with the art of staying warm.

Everything was a lesson. Her childhood had always been filled with broken promises, and that didn't change. But now, when the promised tickets for a Prince concert didn't materialize, he told her to recognize the folly in attachment. He was fond of dramatic actions, such as smashing a potted plant to demonstrate impermanence, actions that kept her on edge, always watching him, always aware of him. She relaxed only when she was with Annie, sitting in her room, listening to music.

There were good times, when Char felt herself to be very fortunate, that she had a life where she was encouraged to connect with spirit, and appreciate the depth and beauty of the world around her. Keith had friends who kept snakes and raptors. He frequently visited them, encouraging Char to get accustomed to the presence of the birds and reptiles. Char loved them all. A baby eagle drew her into complete awe. She spent a whole day sitting in front of a kennel where six young owls were roosting, saved from starvation after the mother owl had died. She happily missed lunch and dinner, and didn't want to go to bed, she was so delighted to be sitting there communing with them, swimming in the pools of their perfect round eyes.

Keith, whose native name was Koheehut, was known in certain circles as a healer. Sometimes people came to the house for his services, and she watched as her stepfather drew out their pain, using his hands in a claw-like formation. The same method worked for her when she had menstrual cramps or a headache. He knew herbs too, using the chanupa (the sacred pipe) with different herbal mixtures for different situations: one to help memory, one for pain, one for grief.

Keith's ability to read minds meant that he automatically knew about any infringement of the rules he set, and he proved that to her often, with passing remarks related to what she was thinking, or what she had just been doing. He taught her how to tap into the energies around them, whether physically manifested or not. It was a skill she easily picked up. As they sat by candlelight at the kitchen table, which was the setting for so much of her training, he touched the wooden surface, and said, "Tell me about who made this."

She put her hands on the table and began to talk, describing the pictures that formed in her mind as she allowed them. "I see a man and a woman working…I see the logger cutting the tree, I hear the saw, I see a helicopter." She paused, her eyes half closed, and he waited. "I hear the diamonds of the sandpaper—*tch tch tch tch*—and I see the miner who mined the diamonds, he's cutting the good diamonds. Then there's the dust from those, and the person collecting the dust…they're making the sandpaper. That takes us back to trees." She talked on, describing the whole lineage of the table, the varnish, and the trees that created the varnish, the lives of all the different trees that went into making the table. "It wasn't just one tree, it was lots of trees, so how could the table not have life force!" She was amazed at the infinite intricacy of the world around her.

From then on, she took great pleasure in sitting at that table. She developed a deep respect for so-called inanimate things, recognizing that whenever there is a gift, there is also a sacrifice. Everything is alive and everything is connected.

One warm day at the house in Wenatchee, Char stood on the front porch admiring the clouds sailing majestically through the branches of the big cedar tree in the yard. Keith came out behind her, putting his arm around her shoulders as he nodded at the beautiful tree, saying, "I can uproot that cedar right now if I want, and you will be able to do the same thing by the time I am done with you. If you can't, I haven't trained you right." She looked at him silently, believing absolutely in his power, and anxious that she wouldn't be able to live up to his standards.

They started with a pencil in a jar on the window sill. For days, she concentrated, desperately willing it to move. When she had finally stopped trying and resigned herself, in tears, to her failure, then it just moved in the cup. She laughed out loud, understanding that you don't *try* to do anything. The *trying* gets in the way.

Keith never made a big deal of her accomplishments. A slight smile flickered across his face when he saw that it had moved, and he nodded, saying, "OK, shithead."

Other medicine people occasionally came by to visit or talk business with Keith. If he wanted privacy he would take them outside, but it was often a social visit and then they would sit around the table in the kitchen, chatting. Char listened, as she sewed some colorful piece of embroidery on a shirt or a pair of pants.

One of the regular visitors was an older woman called Pat. Char warmed to her at once, though she felt somewhat in awe. One day, Pat brought in a little box and handed it to her, saying, "This is for you."

Opening it, Char found a beautiful necklace made with several different kinds of seeds of varying shapes and colors. She gasped in pleasure. Keith, who was sitting watching, said, "It's yours, but you can't wear it for a year." His eyes flickered as he said this, and she understood that it was a power object. Thanking Pat gracefully, she put the necklace back in the box.

Later, in her room, she took it out to admire it again. So perfectly made, such a beautiful piece of natural art. She stood in front of the mirror and held it up to her throat, thinking, *it can't do any harm just to put it on once.* She slid it over her head. As it lay against her skin, sound burst forth inside her. She heard a vast symphony that was much more than sound. She was outside of herself, hearing everything, not just everything that was going on around her, but everything in the world, all of life. Then the necklace burst, scattering seeds all over the room. So bemused by the opening that had occurred inside her, she hardly noticed. She managed to make her way to the bed to lie down. Gradually the intensity of the experience lightened. After a while—she had no idea how long—she got up and methodically searched the floor, picking up each seed, placing them all back in the box. She closed it up and put it away.

She never told anyone what had happened, and no one ever asked. Later she figured they must have known she would put it on.

Keith had altars everywhere around the house—shelves and tables displaying mixtures of herbs, stones, little buckskin bags, crystals, and candles. After her adventure with the necklace, she never messed with anything when he told her not to.

When she had been there a while, Keith took up his old drinking habits. He had little control over his addiction to alcohol, and it began to rule the sanity or insanity of their lives. When he wasn't drinking, he still took Char out on trips to the mountains or the desert, teaching her about Nature, which she loved, even when he imposed some discomfort such as ordering her not to move a muscle for hours. But sometimes he only consumed beer for weeks. Her beloved friend Annie was summarily banned from the house for disobeying him. "She's one of the enemy now, be careful around her, she's not to be trusted," he told Char.

He became obsessed with his own death, lying on the settee in the front room for days with all the curtains drawn, talking only of how he soon would die, and what Char must do when he was gone. Drunk or not, he maintained rigid control over her life. She never knew when he would snap out of his drunkenness to shape her reality in some extraordinary way.

Keith rarely worked, and they lived on a pittance, in a house where the cupboards were often empty. A veteran of the Vietnam War, where he had done two tours, he would frequently scream in his sleep, or get up and wave a gun around, with wide open unseeing eyes. No one could get near him in that state. All Char could do was sit very still and pray, "Oh, Great Spirit, let this be over soon, let this be over soon."

His experiences in Vietnam had left him with little regard for the gift of life. With his familiar enigmatic smile, he told Char that one of his jobs was to kill people. On more than one occasion, he ordered her into the car very late on a dark night, and drove to an isolated place, where he got out, tucking his gun into his pocket, and walked away. Left alone in the pitch black for what seemed like hours, Char tried at first to *see* what he was doing, and then tried not to.

Keith was very attractive to women, and he constantly capitalized on that, with complete lack of integrity. Once, Char answered a knock on the door to find a naked woman standing on the step. Giggling, the naked visitor asked for Keith, in spite of Char's obvious lack of amusement. The most unfortunate aspect to Keith's twisted sexuality was his obsession with teenage girls. Inevitably, as soon as he started drinking, his relationship with his stepdaughter became sexual. He was used to taking what he wanted without asking, and that was what he did with Char. He told her that sex was a way of transferring information to her. He would die soon, he said, he didn't have time to be kind in his teaching.

She was allowed to take drugs, and sometimes she was high on some substance for days. But she clearly saw the negative effect that alcohol was having on Keith, and she knew she wanted no part in that. Her keen awareness of energies unseen by most people did not offer her solace; it only increased her receptivity to the pain around her, especially Keith's. Even in the worst of those years, she had nowhere to turn for help. Keith told her repeatedly and emphatically that she must tell no one about the training, and she believed him. Although her mother, Matilda, turned up occasionally to take her out, Char was always careful to reveal only the most superficial facets of her life with Keith; she knew that Matilda could cause them trouble.

She became increasingly resigned to her fate, understanding that she must deal with this alone, while learning what she could. The illicit sex with her father was a transfer of energy on a literal level; she could clearly see the blue light that passed into him from her. Needing some justification for his unjustifiable behavior, she came to believe this energy was keeping him alive. Escape was out of the question, and in any case, there was no one to turn to.

She could not abandon the man she called her teacher. He was Daddy, he was dying, and he needed her.

Some of his oil paintings—abstract scenery, swirls and lines and curves that spoke a million meanings, splashing color and song—hung around the house. In Char's isolation, those paintings became her friends, an always forgiving source of comfort. One day when she threatened to disobey him by going to a party with some friends, he gave her a black eye, then tore around the house in fury, ripping the paintings down and setting them on fire under the old corkscrew willow tree outside the back door. The party forgotten, Char sobbed, powerless to stop the destruction. He turned to her, unmoved, and said, "You have to learn to let go of your attachment to things, you have to learn to enjoy what's happening in the moment. Enjoy the fire, enjoy the flames."

After three years, aged seventeen, she took a job, taking care of the reptiles in a pet store. She loved this opportunity to be around snakes and lizards all day long. She easily made friends, and was soon offered another place to live. So she moved away, beginning the process of distancing from Keith, though she continued to see him every couple of weeks. She dreamed of him often, and his teachings continued in the dreamtime, where they would talk, or go on walks. Lessons in this arena were just as vivid for Char. Once in the dreamtime, they went to a graveyard to see what death looked like; another time he showed her dismembered bodies. "Losing your head is a very shamanic thing to do, you know," he said, piercing her with those brilliant blue eyes. Char realized he was toughening her up, so she would not balk at something just because it wasn't pretty—an essential ability for any healer.

He died when she was twenty-one. Gradually, the dreams ceased. Some years later, Char got in touch with her anger about the ways she had been used, and worked on transforming that anger. Her unmitigated commitment to wholeness, and the resulting rigorous introspection, have enabled her to heal from her childhood pain, with help from other practitioners. Keith's callous self-centeredness has led her to choose the opposite, to act conscientiously and caringly, now that she is in charge of her own life.

During her years of healing, she had one more dream about Keith: *She knows herself to be dead, lying under an inch of beautiful clear water. She gets up out of her body and walks along a desert pathway, seeing a dead dog, a dead squirrel and other dead animals, thinking to herself how interesting it is to be dead. She becomes aware she is at the top of a magnificent cliff with a bench in front of her, and an eagle soaring above. Keith sits on the bench, facing away from her. He says, "I am so sorry. I am so sorry." With those words, Char becomes the eagle. Her wings are spread wide and feel the support of the air as she turns slowly, majestically, on the spiraling breeze. She looks down into canyons, over rocks, trees, rivers, animals, the whole earth, reveling in the glorious gift of long-sightedness.*

Waking from the dream, she could still feel the eagle, and the presence of her Dad. Understanding it as a visitation, she spoke the words for him, "I know you are sorry."

Keith has become a memory, inlaid with grief that once was anger—learned from, and forgiven.

Part Two

The Early Years of Healing Work

Chapter Four

When Char was only fourteen, Keith arranged a future marriage for her, to a man she never met. In time, she grew tired of waiting. Although she herself didn't really notice, men were frequently attracted to her, not only by her physical beauty but also by the joy that she radiated. After she had worked in the pet store for a couple of months, she began to date a man called Brent. He was a good person, and eventually they got married, living together in Seattle.

With time to spare now that she didn't have to work to pay rent, Char started doing Native American artwork, making pouches, moccasins and shields, and attending powwows, fairs and swap meets, where she could sell what she had made. A friend suggested she take her work to a store called Tribes. Char followed the advice, although very nervous of the response she would get. As soon as she produced her pieces, the owner exclaimed excitedly, "I want this art in my store!"

So her art took off. She did shows, and pretty soon things were selling faster than she could produce them. People started asking for private pieces to help them in their personal growth work, so she made shamanic shields to help in specific ways. This meant they were power objects, demanding an acute level of concentration in the process of manufacture. She was also required to collect things from Nature to be part of them. It brought her great joy to be practicing her spirituality. When the body of a hawk, or a coyote, or some other animal presented itself for her use, she honored it, and listened to the instructions it gave her. She was always aware of the presence of animal spirits, and in these years, she began to relate very closely with her power animals—her own special allies, who gradually became very active in her day-to-day healing work.

Brent wasn't so pleased with her new focus. "When are you going to deal with that raccoon carcass in the basement? It's been there a day and a half! Why is our freezer full of crows and hawks and baby seals? Could we have some food in there some day?" he asked, irritably.

One day, she was sorting through hides in a leather store, preparatory to buying some, when one of the hides spoke to her. "You are to make prayer dolls out of me," it said. Char had never made them before, but she had seen Apache dolls, which are an Apache tradition. She bought the hide and began to work on it, quickly finding that it would give her ongoing instructions. Each doll was different, assuming personalities of its own as it took physical shape. Sometimes she would be making three at one time, but sometimes one would have to be complete before it would allow her to start another. One hide would make six to seven prayer dolls. She could look at a flat hide and see them, as though they were popping out of it. Once, she made a whole tribe of dolls. Each one told her how much to charge. They might say, "The person who is going to buy me needs to spend $230," or "The person who is going to buy me needs to spend $25." Each doll had a name, a story, and a gift, and they were all sold, or given away, before she finished them. Although she only made a total of just over a hundred, they were the most popular item she ever produced. People became quite obsessed with them, and she was asked to show them at the Seattle Art Museum.

Her art kept her busy, but she still wanted to see more of the world from different angles. Pretty soon, in spite of Brent's protests, she got a job as a certified nurse's aide at a nursing home. The second day she was there, an old lady died while Char sat in her room. The air started to glow, with an incandescent golden color that vibrated. Then a tangible white light came out of the dying woman, and expanded into the whole room. Char was astounded and delighted. It was the most beautiful thing she had ever seen. A number of other very sick people died while she worked there, perhaps because she gave them permission to depart. She always saw some kind of accompanying visual; one man had white birds flying out of his chest. As long as she was present for the death and saw the apparition that went with it, whatever that was, then she felt comfortable about it. She only grieved when she wasn't able to be present during the process of dying.

Later she took a job as a bartender, first at the Eagles Club, and then at the Hideaway, which was located in a place called Rat City. It was as big as a postage stamp, and very dark. These were some of the worst biker bars in the city, but Char had no trouble holding her own. If the men got rough or fresh with her, she took it as an opportunity for healing. Since she could see what was truthfully going on for them, she could always stop them in their tracks. She might say, "This affair that you are having, do you really think it's such a good idea?" No matter how angry they were, the men knew better than to mess with her, since she clearly knew truths that they were trying to hide, and they didn't want to give her cause to tell the world. It wasn't an easy environment for her, though, because she could always feel the pain of the unhappy souls who frequented the bar. These were the days before she had learned good boundaries or knew how to protect herself, and she was still trying to fix everyone while she mixed their drinks.

She worked for a while at Tribes, the Native American Arts company that displayed her shields. The owner had a wonderful art collection from indigenous tribes all over the country. It was a great opportunity for her to meet people who accepted her. She began to understand that she didn't need to be so secretive about her beliefs and her abilities. As her spiritual work became more public and began to take up more and more of her time, she grew further apart from her husband. The day came when they agreed to divorce, a painful but necessary step. They always remained friends, and there is still, to this day, a tangible love between them. From then on, however, Char was clear that her spiritual work always took precedence over her relationships.

Brahmari, a woman who gave psychic readings at Tribes, quickly grew close to Char, recognizing her remarkable gifts. She soon picked up that Char was psychic and told her so, but Char didn't want that word applied to her; Keith had always said she should mistrust anyone who called herself psychic. One day, Brahmari explained, "The medicine person in your culture is the psychic in white culture. That's what medicine people do, they're psychic. I've watched you relate to people, that's what you're doing, you're reading them psychically."

At that moment, everything clicked into place for Char, and she started doing readings. When Brahmari showed her the Tarot deck that she herself worked with, Char immediately grasped the imagery and the symbolism that was inherent in the cards. Her friend told her, "Don't read any of the books. You're psychic, just pay attention to your psychic intuition. The books will only mess you up." Of course, Char, with her endless thirst for knowledge, *did* end up reading lots of books, taking whatever they offered of value. But Brahmari's validation of her innate ability to see in psychic realms helped her to trust the inner knowing that never failed her. Gradually, she began to develop her very own style of healing, using images and archetypes from a number of spiritual traditions.

Very soon, Char found herself doing readings professionally, every day, both over the phone and in person. She was good enough that her reputation brought her clients without any advertising. She found her body going through a strange transformation: she felt like she was spinning all the time, and for a few months she threw up daily. A doctor sent her to a psychiatrist, who put her on prescription drugs, which she stopped taking as soon as she found that they interfered with her ability to do psychic readings. Eventually her body settled down. It seemed to have gone through some slow molecular change, in order to let her go into other people's minds, memories, and bodies.

Whenever there was a powwow in the Northwest, Char went to sell her artwork and meet with others who were doing similar work. At one such powwow, she was sewing a moccasin at her table, and since business was slow, she slid off her seat to sit where she was comfortable, on the ground under the table, singing a song that came to her. She was preoccupied enough with the song and the sewing that she didn't notice the pair of legs, hidden in a long skirt, that stopped by the table. Then a wrinkled smiling brown face appeared upside down, saying "Hallo! I heard you singing while I was in the sweat, and I thought to myself, I need to meet that voice!"

This was Barbara Means Adams, a Lakota story teller. They got to chatting, and pretty soon, Barbara found out all about who Char was and what she did. At the end of the weekend, Barbara took her aside, and said, "I am a Lakota elder, and I have a great deal of information that shouldn't be lost, but my children don't want to carry on this tradition. I'm not a medicine woman and I need someone who is, to work with me. I will teach you what I know and we will do groups together: you will do medicine work while I talk and tell stories. I want you to come and live with me."

Char was still young and naïve, and looking for a teacher, so when an elder said, "I want you to come and live with me," she reckoned that meant now. She packed all her bags and moved in, sleeping on a mat beside her new teacher's bed. Since Barbara had no daughters of her own, she was delighted to adopt Char as a daughter and an apprentice. Her life was chaotic, and one of her sons drank a great deal, so it was similar in some ways to living with Keith. But now Char was old enough to make her own decisions, and when things got too much, she left, although she often returned.

When Char first met Barbara, she had been doing readings using the Tarot. In her typically blunt fashion, Barbara said, "Any idiot can use the Tarot and you are not an idiot! If you are going to do readings you need to be using something from Nature." She told her to use gourd rattles. Char started reading from the gourds at a powwow, and although she was initially nervous about how it would work, she was delighted to find it very easy. She rattled the gourd, and then just listened. Little gourd allies, that looked to her just like small people, appeared as soon as she shook it, telling her what the client needed to know. After a while, she found she could read without them, and then she only used the gourds for healing.

Barbara and she led many gourd rattle ceremonies together. That meant lots of road trips, working with people from different cultures, and learning many old Lakota songs. During the circles, while sage smoldered and everyone sang the song that Barbara had taught them, Char went around with the rattle. Assisted by the power of the gourd and the group singing, she could frequently alleviate sickness, or at least uncover its source, which was often emotional. This was when she started doing extraction work, which was a clairsentient experience for her—she would *feel* whatever was going on for the person she was working on, and she would *feel* whatever needed to be removed. She became like an open vessel in those circles, aware of everything. Sometimes she felt like she was lost in a huge vortex of energy. When it was time, Barbara would shift the song to bring in positive energy, and then she would go around the circle a second time, filling the spaces left by the negativity that had been removed.

Although Char was living and training with Barbara, she always took time to spend with her friends, and one of those was Brahmari, whom she had met first at Tribes. One day she was over at Brahmari's house. She sat on the sofa, cross-legged as always, watching Brahmari fold her clothes, when something caught her eye: it was a book, a tableau with a waterstained pink cover, lying on the bottom shelf of the book case. Something about it drew her, and she reached out for it, saying, "What's this book?"

Brahmari glanced up from her pile of washing, and said, "Wait a minute, you can't look at that." She took it from Char's hand, putting it on the top shelf where it couldn't so easily be seen.

Char looked at her in surprise. "Well, what *is* it? What's so special about it?"

Brahmari frowned. "Well, we're not supposed to tell anyone but I suppose it's OK to tell you. You can't read the book until it's finished, though. It's from an entity I've been channeling. He only wants to channel to me. The stuff he's giving me is really cool, but he doesn't want anyone to know about it until the time is right."

It was Char's turn to frown. "Don't you think that's a little strange, that he doesn't want anyone to know about it?"

"Well, no! He just wants to get a bunch of information to me, and I'll put it in book form and then everyone will get to hear it. That's just the way he wants it. It isn't time for it to be revealed yet."

"Hmmm…"

"The information he has been giving me is really great stuff, really cosmic. And some of it is really down to earth, like he says he has a cure for AIDS."

"Well…I'll look forward to reading it when the time is right." Char was uneasy, but she dropped the subject. When Brahmari finished folding her clothes, they had dinner. Although Char had cooked Brahmari's favorite dish, she ate very little of it. As she was clearing away the plates, Char said, "Are you feeling OK, Brahmari? You haven't eaten any of that. You used to love it."

"Mmmm…I'm feeling a little sick."

"Sweetie, you should see the doctor." Standing behind the chair, Char put her arms affectionately around Brahmari's neck, and the woman smiled up at her.

Back in the living room, Brahmari sat down on the sofa, smoking a cigarette, while Char sat opposite her, stroking the cat. She glanced up to remark how soft and fat the stray tabby had become since living here, but the words never got out of her mouth. On Brahmari's shoulder sat a man's head. A putrid green, it was continually turning around and around. He was smiling, not a pleasant smile; he had some teeth missing, and those that she could see were very sharp. He had the eyes of a lizard, and she remembered her father saying never trust a human face that doesn't have human eyes. This face was very solid, very real, terrifyingly real. She thought, *I am hallucinating, this is so bizarre, it's almost like he is sharing a body with her.*

Sensing that something was wrong, Brahmari looked up, and quickly assessed Char's expression. "What are you seeing?"

Transfixed by the awful apparition, Char didn't reply, and Brahmari became agitated. "What is it, Char, what do you see? What are you seeing?"

Char tore her gaze away, searching for words. What was she going to say? *There is a horrible demonic creature glued to your neck?* She took a deep breath, in an effort to sound casual. "I'm just seeing this spirit that is with you."

Brahmari seemed satisfied, and the next time she looked, Char didn't see the entity. But she did not forget about him. Over the next few weeks, Brahmari's physical and emotional health worsened. Gradually she became suicidal, and she began to talk incessantly about wanting to be in a small dark place. One day Char got a phone call from Brahmari's boss at Tribes.

"Char, you need to do something, I don't know what to do! Brahmari seems to be really suicidal, and homicidal too, I don't want to let her drive, she says she wants to drive her car into a brick wall! I've taken her car keys away, but if you can't take care of her, we need to put her in a psych ward."

Char immediately came over. She found Brahmari babbling constantly and making no sense, except for vague threats. Char took her back to Barbara's house, where they locked her in a small room so that she could do no damage to herself or anyone else. Barbara knew what to do: she called Kenny Moses, one of the last of the real West Coast medicine men, and asked him to do a healing.

Kenny had two drummers with him when he arrived. He took Brahmari into the main room, and tied her to a chair in the center. They cleared everything away so he had space to do his work. One of the drummers sat in the corner, starting up with a steady fast beat. Kenny was in trance, with his eyes closed the whole time, walking around the sick woman, talking in his native language as he pulled things off her. Char watched from a safe distance, fascinated at what he was doing, seeing some of it through a haze, in other realms.

The work went on for four or five hours, and the drummers changed over several times, one picking up as the other stopped. When Kenny was finished, and the drummer fell silent, he untied Brahmari, and she stood up, flexing her wrists. Char went to her anxiously, but she smiled and greeted her with a warm hug. She was fine! They all sat down to eat the fried bread and stew that Char and Barbara had made. Char was very relieved that her friend was back to normal and very impressed with Kenny's healing. Although she had no idea how, she knew that she wanted to learn how to do that work herself.

Later she understood that much of what Kenny Moses was doing was what people called a soul retrieval. Nearly five years passed before Char had her own experience of a soul retrieval from a practitioner she was introduced to. The changes she experienced as a result were very exciting to her, so she spent two years doing classes with Sheila Belanger, a local practitioner. When she first asked about the training, Sheila told her, "You already know how to do this work, Char, you don't need me to teach you!"

Although it was true that working in those arenas did come very naturally to her, the teaching was useful. It cemented her relationship to her power animals, Snow Leopard and Raven, it gave her a setting for the work, and it gave her the language to describe what she was doing.

Chapter Five

Char had plenty of friends, so even when she and Brent agreed to live apart, she was never lonely. One of her dearest friends was Claudia. The two of them often hung out at the Brass Connection, a gay bar with regular drag shows. It was easy to be there because none of the men were trying to hit on them. Char first became acquainted with drag queens through the gay boy who had been her foster brother in Chelan, and she loved them. Through her own life experience, she was familiar with their struggles about where and how to fit into mainstream culture. She saw the people in the gay community as powerful "two-spirits" whose power had been eroded as a result of living in a culture that devalued them. She wanted to help to return their esteem to them.

At that time, Pam, a very shy woman living on Whidbey Island, was apprenticed to Char. Pam rarely socialized, since she felt uneasy and insecure in groups of people, but her sister had taken her to Tribes, where Char was working, and had bought Pam a psychic reading. Although the shy woman initially resisted, she was entranced when she finally sat down with Char. No one had ever accepted her with such ease; bathed in the love that Char extended unconditionally to all her clients, Pam felt warmed and healed. Char saw all the people who came to her in their spirit form. In spirit, human failings are irrelevant. She saw everyone's potential, and in Pam's case, that was clearly her psychic abilities. Over a period of six months they gradually became friends, and then spirit told her that Pam should be her apprentice. Pam, of course, felt quite unworthy of such an honor, but her admiration of Char, and her desire to be in that presence, won out over her mistrust of herself.

Every day on her way to Tribes, Char drove by a big rundown apartment building on Cherry St. Although it was in very bad condition, something about the building intrigued Char, and it always caught her eye. One day she saw that a yellow tape was tied across the entrance, branding it as condemned. Grief welled up in her. Then she heard spirit saying: "Saving of this building is a task that will foster love, and you will find it very rewarding."

So Char became the manager of the building, forestalling demolition. Since she'd spent half her childhood in slums, this kind of existence was not alien to her. Of the thirty apartments, only half of them were occupied, and many of the occupants were on crack. One of the toilets had fallen through the ceiling below. The cockroaches were awful. The place was so dirty, it looked like someone had smeared shit on the walls all the way up the stairs, and there were big holes in the plaster. Cleaning it up was a daunting job. But Char had friends. They came to help her, forming work parties that really got things done. They put the toilet back in the right apartment, patched all the holes in the walls, and painted the whole place. All the while they were working, the kids from the apartments were running in and out, mostly in their pajamas, saying, "Char, Char, what are you doing?"

"Cleaning this place up so you don't have to live like this any more!" she replied with a smile.

In places, the cockroaches literally swarmed around the walls, making it look as though the paint was alive. One of the abandoned apartments smelled so bad when Pam and Char entered, that they were both close to gagging. Mustering the courage to look around, they found used diapers lying on shelves and in kitchen cupboards. Pam opened the fridge, leaping backwards as hordes of cockroaches flew in her face. Char instructed her to clean that apartment as part of her apprenticeship, thinking it was a perfect death and rebirth experience. Pam was a good worker as long as she didn't have to deal with people, and she acquitted her duties well. Soon after that, Pete, the owner of the building, paid for the pest control people to come in, and the cockroaches left for good.

The building had become a hangout for people who were down and out, especially alcoholics and drug addicts. Char knew that all the addicts and dealers had to go. The guy in the basement, who was dealing crack, had busted all the windows in a fit of angry paranoia. Nothing changed when she gave him an eviction notice, so she told him in person that he needed to leave. Although he seemed amenable, he simply never left. Char made it her business to know everything that went on, and she knew that his parents came to bring him lunch every day. One morning she intercepted them. After she introduced herself, melting their hearts with her warmth, she said, "You know, I really can't have your son in the basement being so crazy. I've given him an eviction notice but he just won't leave."

Two days later, his parents put him in an addiction treatment center, and Char started work on the basement. It took a long time to fix up, but meanwhile Char's friend Connie had moved in downstairs, her friend Marcie had moved into an apartment on the main floor, and her friend Moni had moved in upstairs, next door to her. Then Roxie, the queen of all drag queens, who did a regular show at the Brass Connection, turned up one day, greeting Char with her usual aplomb. Waving her hand theatrically, she said, "Ah hea' that you are the manager of this apartment building, and Ah need a place to live!"

Char was delighted, and Roxie moved in the following week. Several of the other club regulars followed: Miss Ebony and her boyfriend, then David, then Steven and Camille, who did everyone's wigs. All the gay men would come over and pose for Char, saying, "Girl, how do you like my outfit?" and Char would reply, "I love it, it is so beautiful!" And they *were* beautiful. She loved them with her whole heart.

They also helped to make the building look good. Johnny Moses, a native story teller, had moved in downstairs with his boyfriend, and they made drums, which hung on the walls of their living room, where they were seen through the window by everyone who walked into the building. The tone of the place was profoundly changed.

Char made it quite clear that she wouldn't tolerate drug taking. In the evenings, she gathered her spirit allies, came down the hallway and said to all the folks who were hanging out on the doorstep, "Good evening! Hey, you know, I told you yesterday, you're welcome to visit here, but you can't be using drugs here! *No* drugs, OK?"

Sometimes, when they were really weird and paid no attention to her, she would run at them, and they would back away very fast, scared out of their wits. If they talked back, she would stand up close to them, telling them again and again they couldn't be using drugs here, they couldn't be messing the place up. If they raised their voices, so did she. On some level, she was saying to them, "Hey, you know what, my spirit allies would *love* to escort you out of here!" Although she never said these words aloud, they all could hear them, and knew they'd met their match. As things got better, she sat and chatted with the ones who still came by, always telling them, calmly and firmly, "The rules are, you don't get to use crack, and you don't get to leave beer bottles on the porch!"

There were a few stragglers. Char didn't let anything go. One day, on her way out, she found the front door propped open with a purse. It was now normally left locked, and there was a working intercom for visitors. Looking inside the purse, she saw a crack pipe. So she waited in the doorway, purse in hand. In a little while, a woman came walking down the stairs, glared at Char, and said, "That is my purse!"

"Yes, it is," said Char, without moving.

"I need to have that back!"

Char turned to face her fully. "You know what, you are not allowed to do crack in my building, little girl, you need to go away and never come back with a crack pipe, do you hear me?" She handed her the purse, and never saw her again.

But there was still one crazy, Joe, upstairs, who regularly threw his garbage out of the window into the back garden. She told him very specifically: "It is not OK for you to throw your garbage in the back yard, you don't get to do that any more."

His response was quite reasonable, and from then on, he no longer threw his garbage out of the window. Otherwise his behavior was as crazy as ever. One day he was carrying on, shrieking as he ran up and down the hallway. Char was in her apartment, listening. She realized something would have to be done, but she wasn't quite ready to call the cops. So she asked spirit for help. As she felt the power of spirit surge through her, she could hear all the voices that he was hearing, that were bothering him. She went out into the hallway, and ran shrieking straight at him, doing exactly the same thing he was doing. He stopped, watched her for a minute or two, and said, "You're crazy, what's wrong with you?"

She wasn't making sense, she was just saying what she heard his spirits saying to him. After a little while, he went running into his room, saying, "I gotta get away from you!"

There were several more instances where he started to shriek, and when she mirrored his behavior, he would quiet down and go into his room. One day, hoping for a more permanent resolution, she called 911. As she was explaining what was going on, the dispatcher said in a questioning tone, "Char?"

Recognizing the voice, she realized it was one of her clients. "Patti? Is that you?"

"Char, are you all right?" Patti was very concerned. "Don't worry, I'll send several cars, you'll be safe, I promise you, are you sure you're all right?"

Char was a little embarrassed, since she didn't feel that she herself was in any danger, but several police cars turned up anyway. Joe was in his room by then, so they went in, four big policemen at the front and Char behind. He calmed down pretty quickly when he saw the cops. They were in there long enough for Char to see the contents of his apartment: a mattress, a TV, and all the garbage he had not been throwing out of the window, neatly stacked up his walls.

In the long-term, Joe's behavior didn't improve, and eventually Char had to evict him. The guy she got in his place seemed very sweet, and Char's psychic scan on him came up clean. One day, however, Steven and Camille, who lived downstairs from him, knocked on her door to say, "Char, there are three or four voices, there are different people in there. We can hear him saying he is going to kill himself by jumping off something, then he runs and jumps. He does it all night, we can't sleep."

That evening she went down and listened; sure enough, there were several different voices, and the regular sound of someone running. She left it for a while, hoping he would stop of his own accord, but a few nights later, Steven called to say, "Char, you'd better come, it sounds like he has a little girl in there, and he says he has a gun."

So she called the cops again. They broke into the apartment, with their guns drawn, to find him there by himself. Just like Joe, he had no furniture apart from a mattress and a TV.

She never did get anyone doing well in that apartment. By that time she knew how to do house blessings, which are primarily about removing negative energies. She knew the building needed a blessing, to get rid of the strange spirits that were affecting the inhabitants, but her allies told her she should not be the one to do it, since she wouldn't have enough distance to be able to clear her own home. Pam felt too insecure to do it. Frustrated, Char said, "You can't be insecure, you have been training for a year, you have to do the work!"

No amount of her reassurances (which sometimes came close to bullying) would shift Pam's perception of herself. Char decided to go ahead and do it herself.

They started in Char's own apartment, Pam walking along behind her, holding ground, while Char and her power animals negotiated with spirits, muttering quietly, brushing away stale energy with an eagle feather, clapping her hands along walls and in corners where entities that should have been long gone were still doing their thing. Pam, concentrating on holding energy in the present time and place as a marker for Char to come home to when her journeying was done, opened her eyes wide in alarm when she saw that Char had dropped the eagle feather on the ground. She knew immediately that something was wrong, because Char always treated her tools with absolute respect, and would never discard such a valuable talisman like that. The medicine woman was clawing at her back, and twisting her body in discomfort, drawing deep breaths.

"What's going on, Char? What happened?" Pam anxiously questioned her. It was a few minutes before Char managed to answer, but finally she said, in a strangled voice, "There's something attached to my back, it's like a sword under my shoulder blades...help me get it off!"

It was ensconced well into her body, sending sharp pain shooting down her spine and into her arms, and she was terrified. So was Pam, feeling quite ill-equipped to deal with such a dire emergency. But no other help was available; it was up to her. As Char dug into the skin of her back with her fingertips, trying to pull off the entity, Pam tried to talk to it. Initially she was too upset to connect, but finally it gave her the information that it really enjoyed being in Char's body because it was so warm. So she filled the bathtub with iced water, and Char got into it, with all her clothes on. As she lay shivering in the freezing water, getting colder and colder, so did the entity inside her. At last she felt the pain in her back subside; it had departed. She climbed out of the bath, crying with relief. Pam helped her remove her wet clothes and she lay down in bed, almost immediately falling into a deep restful sleep, with Pam still anxiously watching over her.

In spite of this unpleasant experience, Char did venture to bless the other apartment building that Pete owned, which was also a mess. A water main had burst, pouring water all the way down the stairs. The big metal door at the front was hanging off its hinges, as though a tornado had hit the place. The manager asked her to bless the whole building, so she went methodically through every single room. One entity that lived in the basement seemed to be particularly powerful, and was clearly responsible for a lot of the problems they'd been having. Char had a long conversation with it, saying over and over, "You can't stay here, that is not an option for you, you have to go! Your poltergeisty energy is no longer welcome here!" It finally agreed to go, but she made the mistake of failing to arrange *where* it was to go. She went back to the apartment at Cherry St when she was done, and found that a water main had broken. The poltergeist had left one building, and gone to another. After that, she never forgot to give the entities a place to go when she moved them on.

I didn't meet Char until she was thirty-one, so I was dependent on Char herself and her eclectic selection of friends to tell me about her early years as a practitioner. Claudia, who had known Char closely for over ten years, had many stories to tell. When Char was living in the apartment building on Cherry St, Claudia became her personal assistant, making all her appointments for her, which meant she was responsible for Char's public image. Representing such an unconventional person was not always easy, especially early on in her career. Laughing wryly, Claudia told me, "Char's come a long way. Life with her is never boring, but it's a lot more manageable than it used to be!"

Char was sitting on the floor of her apartment, where she was making a collage of magazine pictures, when a knock on the door disturbed her reverie. The magazine project was intended to help her set intent for future goals, so she was very focused. Since the energy of the visitor wasn't someone she recognized, she considered ignoring it, but she was at a good place to take a break, so she got up to open the door. Two young men stood there, not much more than boys; fresh faced and clean shaven. "Students," she thought, and welcomed them with her wide smile. "Hallo, how are you?" Before they could open their mouths, the cat made a dash for it. "Fuzzy, where are you going? Fuzzy, come home!" She smiled at the slightly bemused visitors, and held the door open wider. "Come in, sit down! I'll be right back, let me just get Fuzzy." She turned her attention back to the cat and said in a more commanding tone, "Fuzzy, come home! You know you don't want to be out there, come on!" Strolling casually back down the stairs, Fuzzy came inside. Char closed the door and picked her up, snuggling her nose into the golden cat's luxurious coat. "Fuzzy, I love you!"

The boys were standing awkwardly inside. "We've come to look at the car for sale," said the blonde one.

"Oh! Oh yes, you must be the ones who called!"

"Yes, we called this morning."

"Well…let me show you the car! Now…where did I put those keys?" Frowning and pursing her lips, she searched around until she unearthed them in a jacket pocket. The three of them walked outside and chatted over the car for a while, then the two boys took it for a drive.

"You will treat it well, won't you?" Char was slightly anxious, as they got in to drive away. "I love this car so much! I wish I could keep it, but I just can't afford it."

Claudia arrived as they were departing. Char gave her a hug and they walked up the steps arm in arm. As they went in the front door of the big apartment building, which was still in a state of disrepair, Claudia wrinkled her nose. "Honestly, Char, this place stinks, I don't know how you can live here! And you're responsible for the whole building! The only good thing you can say about it is that it has parking!"

"Well, I was sent here…spirit told me to be here, to clear out all the bad energy. The building needs healing."

"You've got your work cut out, if you ask me…is that crack dealer still living upstairs?"

"Yes, but he says he's leaving. The guy on the first floor smashed all his windows out last night, and the cops came and got him, so I think we won't be seeing him again. Spirit told me he won't be back. I have some people coming to deal with the cockroaches next week. The woman upstairs has a really bad infestation."

Claudia wasn't finished expressing her disapproval. "You're going to lose some clientele, you know, some people aren't going to want to come here. I've already had one person complain that there was nowhere to sit that wasn't covered in cat hair."

Fuzzy jumped off one of the chairs onto the floor, stalking off with her tail in the air. Char walked into the kitchen to put the kettle on, talking over her shoulder. "I don't know what the problem is. What's wrong with a little cat hair? If they don't like me, they can find someone else to read them! There are plenty of psychics around."

It was Claudia's turn to shrug. "Oh well, it's your life! Here, I brought your schedule for tomorrow. You've got a full day, six readings."

Char took the paper from her, putting it on the table without looking at it. Seeing that she was a little miffed, Claudia put her arm around her. "I don't mean to make you feel bad, I know you're a brilliant reader, and you're certainly good enough that you'll continue to get clients."

Char looked slightly mollified, but continued to frown as she said, "Well, I think the healing of this building is a lot to do with my own personal healing, and I really need to do it. There's a limit to how much effort I can make to put people at ease. I'm already trying really hard to be on time, ever since you complained about me being late!"

"Yes, and I really appreciate that, and you are getting much better. I know time is really difficult for you. It's just that I feel responsible because I'm doing your bookings and I recommend so many people to you. Everyone I've spoken to has been really impressed with your readings, they think you're wonderful, and it's true, you are!"

They smiled at each other. Just then there was a knock at the door. "Oh, that'll be the boys! Come in!"

The boys trooped in, the blonde one handing Char the keys. "Well, did you like her? What do you think?" she asked. "Did she go well for you? Oh, I'm gonna miss my little car! I love that car!"

"Well, we are interested, we'd like to talk to you about it." It was the one with the flowery shirt who spoke, his contained demeanor in stark contrast to Char's.

Char grinned from ear to ear. "Well, sit down, we're just making some tea, you want some?" They both declined, but Claudia and Char made some anyway. Soon they were all four sitting around the table cluttered with papers, which Char scooped up and put in a pile on the floor, to make room for the tray with the flowery tea set. She and Claudia smoked cigarettes, sipping strong tea from little china cups as they talked.

After a short discussion, Flowery Shirt said, "Well, we could offer you $500 now and the rest in two days. Would that work for you?"

"Lemme ask spirit." Char tipped her head sideways, staring into the corner for a moment. Then she turned back, smiling. "OK! Spirit says that's just fine!" She laughed, pleased. The boys both looked nonplussed. Blondie opened his mouth, closed it again, and then said, "Did you say *spirit*? What does spirit have to do with it?"

"Oh," Char waved her cigarette in the air, "I don't do anything without consulting spirit. They tell me what to do. I always regret it when I don't follow their advice." She laughed again, pouring herself some more tea. Claudia explained.

"Char's a psychic. She does readings for people, and talks with spirit and with dead people. She's very good!"

"*Dead* people?" Blondie raised his eyebrows and shook his head.

"Yes, you know, if someone has a relative who has recently died, Char can contact them to pass on messages."

They both looked doubtful. Flowery Shirt said, "The only dead person I'd wanna talk to is Nikola Tesla. He was really smart."

"I've never heard of him, what did he do?"

"He was an inventor, he did a lot of work with electricity. He was a really cool guy. He used to do these experiments where he would let electricity flow through his body to light lamps."

Claudia was just reaching for the ashtray when they all felt the atmosphere begin to sizzle. Within seconds the room was thick with presence, vibrating with electricity. She felt her hair literally standing vertically away from her head, as though a current was flowing through her. "Wow! He's here! What a powerful person!" She glanced around as though expecting to see him, but there was nothing visible to normal sight. The boys were also looking around, their eyes as big as saucers.

Char was the only one who seemed undisturbed, although her hair was also standing out from her head. Tapping out her cigarette, she turned to face the center of the room. She spoke into space, with a calm but serious tone. "You know, I didn't invite you here, and you have to go. You can't just show up here, that is *not* how this works. You have to go now."

She turned back to sip her tea, smiling at the boys. Flowery Shirt was already standing up, making ready to leave. "Well…er…we gotta go. Come on, John." He shoved the check at Char as he backed away from her. "We'll get the car on Tuesday." They were across the room in a few quick strides, and the door closed behind them before the atmosphere had quite returned to normal.

At the requests of various friends and acquaintances, Char began to teach classes. During the five years since she left Keith, she had studied a number of spiritual practices, and because she already had such an excellent grasp on what it meant to be in touch with spirit, a great deal of knowledge came to her easily. What she found useful, she integrated into her personal practice. She understood that the Tarot, especially as analyzed by Angeles Arrien, was a particularly powerful tool for self-growth.

This class was her second in a series. The women began to trickle in and made themselves comfortable, taking their shoes off and sitting cross-legged on cushions on the floor, in a circle around the small altar. Char greeted each person with a smile and a hug as they arrived. Today they were learning about the archetype of the Fool, the first of the Major Arcana of the Tarot.

When everyone was ready, Char sat down and said a brief prayer, that today's lesson would be taught and learned with integrity, and contribute to the highest good of all. Everyone had their own copy of the Thoth deck, the card of the green clad smiling Fool sitting in front of each student already. Char began to talk, while some of the students took notes, and others watched.

"The Fool…the Fool is the trickster, his element is air, he is associated with the planet Uranus, and his color is yellow. He is symbolic of Great Spirit's clown. He represents childlike innocence and joy. The Fool has no fear, so he teaches us about courage. Look at the tiger gnawing on his leg, he's not paying any attention, he isn't distracted by fear."

When she had talked for a while, she said, "OK, so now we're going to journey to the sound of the drum, with the intent of discovering how can we work with principle of *no fear*, asking, what can I do to experience a state of courage in my life, and be playful? Who am I when I am being the Fool, what am I looking like with no fear, where is my courage? How have I lost my courage, in what ways is my courage being undermined? These are the questions you need to find answers to."

She picked up the drum, running her hand gently over its surface. People started preparing themselves, making a space to lie down.

"When I start drumming, you will find a canoe waiting to take you wherever you are going, or if that doesn't work for you, perhaps you will find a hole in the ground, or a cave to go through. Do whatever works for you. When it's time to come back to this reality, I'll change the drumbeat like this." She demonstrated. "OK, are you all clear about what you are doing? Any questions?"

Everyone seemed ready, so she began hitting the drum. Immediately the fast beat reverberated through the room, filling up every corner. She let her arm take over and settled into it, consciously holding the space to keep her students safe, watching while they journeyed.

At last she allowed the sound to die away, placing the drum carefully against the wall behind her. Gradually the women came back with sighs and stretches, sitting up to scribble furiously in their notebooks. She gave them several minutes to write, and then looked around with a smile. "So, did everyone have fun? Does anyone want to share what happened?"

Claudia put down her pen. "I will!" She grinned broadly. "That was a great journey! I always feel so safe journeying with you, Char, I don't know, I just feel as though you are taking care of us. As soon as you started drumming, I saw him, the Fool, he was flowing through the air trailing stardust. Then I was in the canoe, my feminine guide on the left and my masculine guide on the right—he was this teacher I had when I was in India, called Babaji, he's passed over now. He was there surging ahead, and the Native American woman who represented the feminine was holding back. So the masculine side was all go, and the feminine was saying, 'Ohhhh, brakes on!' The canoe was going round in circles!" Everyone laughed at the image. "Finally they joined hands and arms and worked together. We went to an island, listening to the music of the drum, and there was the house of the Fool. I asked about courage and he showed me men warring: he said when men go to war, they are not afraid, even though their bodies are, because they are concentrating on their objective and they are absolutely committed to that objective. So commitment and concentration drive out fear. If you are concentrating on what you are doing, there is no room for fear, it is just the body that is afraid for its safety, not the self. He showed me an image of hiding in an earthquake, to illustrate that you can get out of the way when there is physical danger, but it's not a lifetime thing, it's just for the moment. Fear is there to alert you when there is immediate danger, that's its purpose." She hesitated and peered at her notebook, muttering, "Hmm, can't read my own writing. Oh, yes, so courage is about trusting yourself and your intuition, and believing in yourself. He showed me a symbol of a yellow lotus; that's the symbol of courage for me. He showed me that I need to learn to *trust*, my fear comes out of lack of trust. He says I go in circles when I mistrust my masculine self, and I'll be able to move forward when the masculine and the feminine sides of me can work together rather than fighting." She looked up, smiling around the circle of attentive faces. "That's pretty much it. So I learned that when I concentrate, pay attention and commit, then fear cannot move in."

There were murmurs of appreciation, and Char nodded, smiling. "Claudia, that's great! It's very appropriate for you." She let a comfortable silence settle before she spoke again. "Anyone else want to share?" She glanced around, catching Marie's eye. "Yes? OK, go ahead!"

Some of Char's clients only want to know who they are going to marry or what dresses they should buy at Nordstrom's, but every now and then someone really special turns up. One such person was Lawrence, a very sweet man, who first came to Char shortly after she moved out of the apartment building on Cherry St into a small house on the city outskirts.

When Char is reading a person, she usually meets her client's guides, or allies—everybody has at least one. Lawrence's allies were two men and a woman, who appeared to be in a library. Their clothes were from the nineteen twenties: the woman was almost always wearing a hat, with a pretty brown dress, very stylized and elegant. One of the men didn't talk much, he just nodded or shook his head, whereas the other man seemed to express opinions for all of them. Lawrence himself was beautiful, with an innocence about him that barely disguised the underlying quality of wisdom. He glowed with a warm white light. Char immediately saw that he was a healer at heart, and that he would only be truly happy when he was working with those healing abilities that were naturally his. Her task, then, was to bring him gently to his own conscious awareness of that.

He visited her after he moved to Seattle in 1993, when he was just starting to come to terms with the shattered-ness of his life. Because he found her input so useful, he had a series of readings. He experienced his time with her as cathartic and cleansing, even when the words or the meaning didn't seem relevant (and later he nearly always found that they *were* relevant). A spiritual re-set button was automatically pushed while he was with her. Even though she was anything but pure and celibate—she smoked and cussed and had sex, and sometimes drank—he felt that she was absolutely in the presence of god. Through her example, he understood that everyone can be in the presence of god on their own terms. He was empowered to do what he needed to, in order to be a consciously spiritual person, following a spiritual path.

She often told him about things that came to pass, which were crucial for him, but what really threw him onto a path of healing was meeting his father, who had died when he was fourteen. He had never made a connection with his grief; he didn't really know how to feel it, much less express it and let it move on. In that first reading, the undeniable presence of his father's spirit was a powerful experience for him. After that, Char was a constant companion for him in healing his stuck grief. She always found exactly the right mixture of caring and carefree, and he came to trust her implicitly.

He gradually developed his own ability to connect with the non-physical realms. During one reading, as she turned to his guides to get the answer to his question, he heard the guide talking to him in his head, just split seconds before she said the exact same words. He had always known, on some level, that he had three guides, but he had never really trusted his intuition. Through Char, he was able to acknowledge that those voices in his head never lied. Sometimes the answers they gave were so *out there* that he didn't know how to trust them, but with Char's encouragement, he learned to do so. She said, "They adore you, and they have never guided you wrong."

He knew it was true. She taught him to find his own answers, by listening to his own guides.

Char told him he should start giving astrological readings. Although he had studied astrology in great depth, his first response to her suggestion was, "That's crazy, what am I supposed to do—hang out a shingle saying I am an astrologer, and people will just come and pay me to give them readings?"

And she said, "Well, yes."

So he did, and was quite successful at it. But he found that he didn't have the same spiritual stamina as Char, and he couldn't do that many readings, back to back. With further advice from Char, he took a job at Amazon.com, in order to pay to study acupuncture, which served his long-term dream of being a healer. In time, he began to practice as an acupuncturist, using his psychic gifts to assist in his diagnoses. Once again, Char succeeded in doing what she set out to do with all her clients: she opened the door to the realization of his heart's desire.

When Brahmari became very sick with AIDS, Char took care of her once a week until she went into the hospice. One night, Char got home very late after being out with a friend. The longhaired golden cat sitting just inside the door looked up at them, meowing, as they entered the apartment.

"Fuzzy, what's the matter? Are you pleased to see me?" Char went into the kitchen, putting her bag down on the table, and Fuzzy followed her, chirping and meowing. Char knelt down to stroke her, and the cat arched her body against the medicine woman's hand, then moved away and walked around the table, still talking. Char frowned. "What's up, Fuzzy? Are you telling me something?" she asked, watching the cat wend its way around the table legs. She stood up, hitting the button on the message machine as she took a cigarette from the packet that Maureen offered her.

"Fuzzy seems to think I should check my messages," she said.

The machine whirred and clicked, then a voice spoke, "Char, this is Margot. Brahmari is not expected to live through the night, so you need to come now."

Char took a deep drag on her cigarette. As the machine clicked off, she nodded slowly, saying, "OK, I guess it's finally time."

"Finally..." Maureen took her hand. "Do you want me to drive to you to the hospital?"

"No, it's better if I take my car, cuz I dunno how long I will be there," said Char decisively. "Knowing Brahmari, she won't die quickly!" She laughed, as she went into her room, rummaged for a few moments, and came out with a book in her hand: it was *Women Who run with the Wolves*. "She always loved this book, maybe she will want me to read to her."

At the hospice she walked up the steps, and told the sleepy receptionist she was here to see Brahmari. Since it was so late, the lighting was turned down, making the corridor silent with shadows. Two women, friends of Brahmari's, were standing outside number three.

"How is she?" asked Char.

The smaller one spoke, "Not good. The doctors say she won't last the night."

Char nodded, opening the door. Brahmari lay with her eyes closed, her face gaunt and stark, her breath coming in short shallow gasps. The dark stillness of the last stages of the disease had taken over her body. Two people sat by the bed, two others stood talking quietly in a corner. In another corner stood a happy warm being, almost androgynous and yet feminine, wearing a cloak of rainbow colors, reminiscent of a person dancing with scarves. It smiled, waving at Char, and she smiled back, feeling a surge of excitement. She knew this beautiful being was Brahmari's death. Without words, she said, "I am so happy to see you, you are so beautiful!" The being laughed.

Margot came over to hug Char, her face somber. Brahmari's mother was there, as usual not a hair out of place, though her panic pervaded the room as she paced to and fro at high speed. Her breath was short and shallow, somewhat like Brahmari's, but noisier. She greeted Char with a few inane words, and Char disguised her distaste, although she was thinking, *you are the last person I would want around me while I was dying*. The woman who was sitting on Brahmari's right moved away to let Char near the bed, and she stood there, setting the book on the covers.

Now it was as though there was no one else in the room. She took Brahmari's hand, though it had no life, and kissed it, holding it between both of her own. "Oh, Brahmari …Brahmari…" Tears rolled down her face. "I am so sorry, so sorry…I hope you'll be happier where you're going. Goodbye, Brahmari. Some day, when I write the book, I will say good words about you." She bent over, kissing Brahmari's cheek. Replacing the bony hand on the covers, she sat down, taking a deep breath to calm herself. "Look, Brahmari, I brought *Women Who Run with the Wolves*. I thought I would read you a story for your journey." As she picked it up, Brahmari's breath stopped for a long moment. Then a short shallow gasp; another long pause; another short shallow gasp. Char put down the book to pick up the lifeless hand again. Brahmari's mother rushed over and rushed away.

"What's happening? Call the nurse, call the nurse! What's happening?"

Char said calmly, "It's OK, she's dying."

Margot came and stood behind her, a hand on her shoulder. Within a minute, Brahmari's body was still and soul-less. As soon as it was done, Char moved away from the bed, and Margot followed her outside. In the corridor, they hugged each other, Char crying openly. "She was waiting for you to say goodbye," said Margot.

"Yes, I know." Char wiped away some tears, and they went into the little waiting room. Char wanted to be gone, now that there was no reason for her to be there, but she was crying too hard to be able to drive. She was grateful for Margot's presence. People came in and out, talking quietly, in the way one is supposed to when someone has just died. There was a general air of relief now that it was finally over. Several people commented that it was obvious Brahmari had been waiting for Char.

At last, pulling herself together, Char left to go home. Driving away from the hospice, she was aware of the rainbow being dancing above her car in a swirl of color, and Brahmari singing, "Oh, I'm so happy, soooo happy, I'm soooo happy!"

Char laughed with pleasure at knowing that it was good. Out loud she said, "That's good, Brahmari, that's good, and I am very glad for you, but now you have to go and do what dead people do!" To her great relief, the rainbow being faded, and within a couple of blocks it was completely gone.

Part Three
Coming into the Fullness of her Healing Powers

Chapter Six

Char can frequently help to find missing people—alive or dead—because she can so easily connect with an individual spirit. When she looks at someone's picture, or holds some personal belonging, she can immediately be there, talking to her or him. The spirits she contacts in this fashion don't usually give an address—that's a little too much physical reality for them—but she might be able to see where they are and what they are doing. They might show her a store, or a church, some kind of landmark, or they might give her a map of the city with a hotspot on it. A person's spirit often wants to be found, because it wants to connect with humans, even when the physical self, that is afraid of dying or of being hurt, might be very wary.

Molly, a policewoman who was a good friend, dropped in on Char quite often, since the house on 12th Avenue was close to her beat. On one occasion, the policewoman brought a picture of a man they were looking for. Char studied the photo for several minutes, frowning and muttering quietly to herself, then said, "I can see where he is, it's really dark…he's not making any sense, let me ask spirit." There was another pause as she stared unseeingly at the wall. "Spirit says it is a few blocks east of here." She turned away and walked in a small circle with her head down, the photo in her hand. But she couldn't connect clearly enough between the realms. She shook her head, and said to Molly, "I'm sorry, this guy is so confused, he doesn't have a sense of what he is doing, or what's happening, or where he is. I can't get anything clear."

Molly shrugged, smiling. "Doesn't matter, I wasn't expecting much anyway, just showed it to you on the off chance!" She got up, ready to leave, but Char stopped her.

"Wait a minute, I'm getting an image…" she looked off to the left, frowning, and then continued. "It's someone who is already dead, and you're going to find him. He's a suicide, and he just came to me because he thinks it would be nice to prepare you for what you're going to see."

That evening, as Molly cruised through the University District, she got a call from the dispatcher to go and check out a car that appeared to be abandoned nearby. She found it in the far corner of an unused lot, hidden behind a brick wall. As she got out of her car, she remembered Char's warning, and steeled herself. Sure enough, in the swathe of bright yellow that her flashlight cast through the dark window, she saw a man's body lying across the front seat. Though there were no signs of blood, he was clearly dead, the skin already slightly puffy and gray as it began to swell. She picked up her radio to call for help.

Another time, she left a message on Char's machine. "Char, there's a rapist we've been warned about, we think he's attacked several women in the Seattle area. I'm not asking you to look for him specifically but if anything does come up, let me know."

Char was busy, and didn't have time to give it her attention right then, but that night, when she was trying to sleep, images of the rapist kept crowding into her mind. She found herself in his house, in a dingy kitchen with a yellow counter, and lots of pictures on the walls. She saw the neighborhood: he lived in Ballard. He kept growling, like an animal, all the time she was in his house. Then she was walking on the street next to him, and he became friendly, as though he felt safer having her around once they were outside. They didn't exchange any identifiable words, but a clear knowing settled over her, like a sheet on her skin as she lay in bed. They were about three weeks ahead in time, and he was getting ready to accost another woman. She could see the woman who was going to be attacked, although there was something strange about her, which she couldn't pin down. Seeing a dumpster in an alleyway, she knew it was in Fremont, and that Molly was going to meet the rapist there.

Finally, bombarded with all this information, she got up out of bed, grabbed the tape recorder and spoke into it. The next day she gave the tape to Molly. Three weeks later, the policewoman told her the man had indeed tried to rape someone, who turned out to be a transvestite. And a few days after that, Molly did meet him in an alleyway, next to a dumpster, although he got away. They caught him shortly after that.

Lee was a private investigator. The first time she came to Char, she had a very business-like list of specific questions about a man who had been murdered. Char tried to concentrate, but neither she nor spirit were responding easily to Lee's professional attitude, and she wasn't getting anywhere. Finally she said, "Lee, you gotta lighten up a bit, this is a spirit thing! Interrogations don't work!"

Lee got the idea: she laughed and relaxed. Then Char was easily able to contact the dead person she was inquiring about, but he wasn't interested in talking about how he had died, only what it was like being dead and how much he disliked it. She couldn't get any clear or useful information out of him. "I'm sorry," she said, shrugging. "Sometimes dead people are just like that, they are completely self-absorbed and don't want to listen to my questions at all, they just want me to listen to them."

A few months later, the PI came about a young woman called Lisa who had been killed in New York a couple of months previously. The police said it was a suicide, and the investigator was employed by her family because they didn't believe she had killed herself. Lee brought Char a box of sheets saturated and stiff with Lisa's blood, which Char stuffed in a closet until she had time to deal with them. When she pulled the box out a day or two later, she was immediately struck by the wonderful smell of roses that wafted from it, and she remembered how the blood of a saint is said to smell like roses. So she thought this girl must be something special. When she met Lisa in spirit form, she did indeed find that the dead woman was delightful.

She was gorgeous looking, with black hair, and smooth pale skin. She turned up first in a yellow dress, but changed her clothes more than once during the reading—not something Char often sees a dead person do. She chatted easily, telling Char about times she had spent with people she had known, and the friends she'd had in human form. She was coming up with names and landmarks, which was very unusual for a spirit. She would say, "Let's see, I was in New York for several days. That was in September, the fall, the leaves were turning, and I was hanging out with this Italian guy." Char was impressed.

The detective wanted to know whether there were any drugs in the house where she had died, and if so, where were they kept. Char didn't think Lisa would be able to answer such a concrete question, but she asked anyway, and to her surprise she got a clear response. "There was a piece of gypsum board cut out in the back of the closet in the bedroom. We took that out, put the drugs in, and put the gypsum board back to hide the hole."

"Well, that sounds pretty stupid," said Char, thinking it would look obvious.

"No, it's not, it worked!" replied Lisa, indignantly. So Char told the detective, who later went to the house in New York to check it out. Sure enough, she found the place Lisa had described, where the gypsum board had been cut out and could be removed, although the drugs were already gone.

Lisa said her boyfriend had killed her. There were several reasons why he did so: she broke up with him, and he was jealous and angry. She clearly loved him, and didn't feel a need for him to be punished. They couldn't nail him anyway, because there was no evidence. After Lisa's family—her parents, sisters, and brother—listened to a tape of the PI's session with Char, they came to Seattle to get a reading, so that they could talk with her. It was deeply moving for them to have the experience of relating to her again, even though she was no longer in physical form. They were all able to come to a place of peace and acceptance about her death.

Lisa was an exceptionally easy and fun spirit to relate to. Doing this kind of work is usually not so pleasant, because the spirits Char is dealing with are frequently troubled, but nowadays she only occasionally experiences distress at what she witnesses in another realm. She's able to keep it fairly factual, so that she doesn't *feel* it. She has learned to distance herself when necessary, knowing that her clairvoyance doesn't *have* to include clairsentience. When she was younger, she felt everything, and the stress of that had been damaging to her, so she learned that it is imperative to have detachment. Even now that she is older and wiser, it's sometimes a big deal going to the mall, or any place where there are a lot of people. She calls in her allies to protect her if she needs to, and she practices sending everyone joy, before *they* can send *her* something negative. Then her whole day is peaceful.

Sometimes someone who has committed a murder comes for a reading. The first time she found herself sitting opposite someone with an image of the person he had killed shimmering in the air beside them, she was very unsure how to handle it. *Why is he coming to a psychic? Does he think I am not going to notice?* Spirit reassured her, saying, "This person knows he has done something very wrong, and he wants to learn to act with compassion." Knowing that she could not afford to take responsibility for other people's sins, she saw that her job was to help him become a better person. She let spirit do the talking, they knew what words to choose.

After years of practice, Char knows when someone is ready to die. She sees the future, to the left, shining brightly, with expanses of flowery fields, and golden light, filled with sweets and honey. It is always indescribably, exquisitely beautiful. She knows that someone's healing is sometimes the process of dying, and she, Char, is not in a position to make a judgment about what others should do or should not do. But when it is someone who has come for a reading, she'll talk to her or him about it, since the client usually needs to talk about death if it is looming, especially if she is suicidal. Spirit is very clear and to the point: "You made this choice years ago, and it is still a choice, you can change it. How are we going to lose this coffin? You can choose a life wish instead of a death wish."

In this way, she tries to show people that they *can* make positive changes, no matter how radical. One of Char's greatest gifts is teaching people to take responsibility for their own lives, and their own choices. She has told me many times, and I believe it to be absolutely true, that no matter what the problem, we can always choose a path of happiness.

Neesha was one of Char's regular clients. She owned a home for the elderly, and had questions about the people she took care of. When she came for a reading, she was always a little late, and her speech was hurried. Even Char's easy manner could not allow her to relax. She was holding a great deal of pain that made it hard for her to sit still, because she was always shifting her body around the pain, even though it was emotional rather than physical.

Her husband had unexpectedly hung himself just as they were moving house. A week later, his brother had followed suit. Within a year his mother, who lived down the street, had also died. Now Neesha, her two sons, and her daughter-in-law were living in the house she had bought with her husband, where he had never lived. All was not well: the daughter-in-law had called Char, asking for help, concerned about the older woman. So now Char was sorting her tools for a house blessing, walking around her apartment, quietly humming to herself, pausing to stroke one cat and speak warmly to another, as she picked up the eagle wing, the sage, the abalone shell, and other things that called to her.

The door opened and Storme, Char's apprentice, came in, with a big smile and a quiet hallo.

"Good morning, Storme!" Char glowed, picking up her bag. They headed out to the truck and Char settled back into the passenger seat, as two small dogs jumped over both of them, excited and irrepressible. They traveled with the windows open, the warm air pressing Char's hair back from her cheeks and almost forcing her eyes closed as she put her head out into the streaming wind. The clouds were building majestically, hiding the white peak of Mt. Rainier. They followed the highway until they were well out of Seattle. Little was spoken, for they were both preparing themselves, already aware of the spirits they were about to meet, already communing with their power animals, who would do the work.

They drove between two white pillars onto a circular driveway. In spite of the size and setting of the house, the garden was clearly unkempt, the lawn in front unevenly green from recent rains, not from any intentional irrigation. As they got out of the car, Char concealed herself in the feathers and bones of her allies.

The sons were absent, so there were only the daughter in law and the mother. Amrita's hair was long and straight, neatly tied back; Neesha's was irresistibly curly, but long and wild. Both of them had brown skin and dark hair, and beautiful dark eyes, lit with the spirits of India. Char felt honored to be working with people from a country so deeply spiritual.

Before they began, Char strolled around the building, melting into the shimmering forms of her allies, the smoke of a cigarette trailing around her. The main room of the house, which should have been the hub of the building's energy, was strangely stark. Two paintings hung on the wall above the fireplace: English landscapes, left there by the previous owner. An ornate straw hat, decorated with flowers by the previous owner, still hung on the hat stand. It was a home that no one who was now alive liked or wanted, filled with shattered dreams, with hopes that were long out of date, changed irrevocably by both expected and unexpected death.

They went into one of the living rooms, with its high ceiling and off-white walls, somehow cold, although it could have been warm. In the center of the room, they built an altar out of the pieces that Char and Storme had brought. The two women had nothing to put in it. They both seemed uneasy. In a quietly tense voice that sometimes lapsed into a whisper, Neesha spoke of acquiring this dream house from a recent widower, who had built it for his dying wife. He was broken by his wife's lost battle with cancer. The house had been erected in grief, and anticipated loss, for someone dying, and now it remained a place of death. Huddled in her chair, Neesha gazed down at the carpet as she spoke of the adjoining land where she had previously lived, and barely audibly described how she found her husband's body hanging in the barn. Abruptly, the wedding feast she had prepared for a cousin, elaborate with Indian spices (Char smelled the cumin, cardamom, and cinnamon in her thoughts), was transformed into a feast for her husband's wake. Now, Char was aware of the husband, dead, yet very much here in the present, more so than the wife who survived him.

It was Amrita's turn. She spoke of moving her mother-in-law's belongings from the old house to this one. Since living here, she'd had trouble sleeping and she'd had strange and frightening dreams she could not recall, except that they were filled with grief and pain. Lightly, she told of her father being run over by a bus in India. She was more alive than her mother-in-law, but a quiet desperation hung around her, telling how the presences in this building were weighing her down. An old sadness had attached itself to both women. Char felt the people walking through their minds, the interference from the past in this beautiful empty house that was, to her, so evidently full of energy without physical form. She understood what wasn't said: their feeling crowded and not knowing why; the low-lying depression that gripped them both; the constant almost-seeing a form, by the stove, through the hall, or in a window when outside tending to the untended yard; the loneliness fed by something they couldn't put their finger on. All her senses felt the invisible ears listening, attentive to their own stories. Although the circle of solid embodied beings was small, she felt it as huge, so strong was the presence of unseen beings.

They began to move through each room, Char apparent to physical eyes but shielded by her power animals from the entities she was dealing with.

Some of the rooms were almost empty, others sparsely furnished. Char met the previous occupant of the house in Amrita's bedroom, in the mirror above the bed. Intrigued by the life of the daughter in law, she was filtering herself into her dreams, wanting a companion to assuage her loneliness. She was coughing lightly, worrying at the things around her, fussing with the blonde hair that had been her pride and joy until chemotherapy made it betray her.

"This house is my life and my dream," she replied, almost aggressively, when Char's allies suggested she leave.

"Fear of life and death no longer serves you," Char said, "but my spirit allies can help if you desire."

The dead woman pondered the offer, comprehending that staying here was not going to bring her the joy she sought, although she couldn't understand why not. "Yes," she said, "I would like to go."

Raven and Snow Leopard guided her sweetly out of the home, transforming her illness and anger into pure spirit as she entered a chariot pulled by a graceful swan, and was carried into other realms.

The husband was still moving about as though living, in the bed, in an overstuffed chair, in the den, still checking on his children in their rooms, still attached to a claim in the past. He spent most of his time in the younger son's room, just watching. Char told him, "You can visit this place, but you must allow others to care for your family." He ignored her, but a tall sweet man came to him, and calmly persuaded him to move forward, prying him away from his sadness and the low hum of anger that hung around him.

In a room with only an elaborate chandelier and one twin bed, an older woman stood waiting for her son to come home, a hopeless quest since he, too, was dead. Gazing at the trees outside, or perhaps the circular driveway, she paid no attention to Char's allies until they addressed her. "It's time to go," they said gently. Absently, listlessly, she followed their directions.

Amrita's father was there too, eager to connect with his daughter, assured of his right to do so. "I am so hungry," he said, "Tell my daughter I love her cooking, tell her I need to eat some of her good food." His expression of love for her was so stern. Char knew it was the love of a rigid and obstinate man, but a caring father.

"You are used to being hungry, but you are not really hungry," her allies told him. Their insistence overcame his initial resistance, though he seemed sad as he climbed into the arms of his angel.

Later, going over what had happened, Char told the daughter of his stern "I love you," and she laughed a sad laugh.

"He was a gruff man," she said, sighing. With gratitude, Char silently honored her allies for their skills, seeing that his departure had taken the most of the pain of his death from Amrita's young heart.

Trying to hide her ongoing anxiety, Neesha asked, "Will things get better now?"

Char and Storme looked at each other, knowing that although the house blessing had removed the hands that were clutching at her, she still had to make the decision to walk away from death and grief.

"I can't tell you that," said Char, with soft warmth. "It's up to you, you have to decide to take responsibility for your own happiness. You need to infuse this house with life. Get rid of all the things that belonged to the woman who lived and died here before you, and fill the space with whatever brings you joy. You must decide to let the past go and move on."

Spending so much time dealing with other peoples' problems, and being so much at ease with spirit, Char can exist for long periods in other realms, ignoring her own needs. Every now and then, she needs time alone, to refuel her batteries and attend to her own issues.

She chooses different places for these retreats. On this occasion, Yemaya, the ocean goddess, was calling to her, so she found a beach where the waves rolled onto the sand on one side, and the woods sprang up on the other. She didn't know the area, but it had spoken to her when she came looking, a few days earlier. She walked until she found a spot that felt exactly right. Putting down her bag, which contained her journal, water and a blanket, she made herself comfortable, sitting in the sand with the long grasses around her.

The morning sky was clear, the sun warm. She decided to sit in each of the four directions for a while, starting in the east, which meant facing the woods. For a while she watched the breeze making the branches dance, enjoying the feel of the sun on her skin, and her naked toes in the sand. She felt the presence of another human before the man in khaki appeared out of the woods a couple of hundred yards away, carrying a rifle over his arm. A golden retriever was running through the grasses with its nose to the ground. Catching her scent, the dog switched direction abruptly, caught sight of a human sitting, and bounded up to her, obviously delighted. She laughed and petted him, as he sniffed all around her, wagging his tail. She knew the dog was not supposed to do this, he was a hunting dog. She could feel the man was annoyed, not just because of the dog, which returned to him when he whistled, but because she was there. His thoughts matched hers: *what are you doing here, when I want to be alone?* They watched each other, she sitting on the sand, and he on a log in the tall grass, the dog beside him. For a moment, she was alarmingly aware that she was alone and he was carrying a rifle. Then she thought about going hunting with her dad. *East is the place of illumination. What is there here to be illuminated?* It dawned on her that Nature is what brings her vision; her dad was irrelevant. She had always associated being in Nature with Keith because he was the one who had taken her to those places—the forests and mountains where they camped and held ceremonies, the valley where she sat for hours watching countless butterflies flutter around her, the waterfall where the ravens nested, the streams where they panned for gold, the river where they fished, the delightful scent of the fields of camass where she played when she was younger, the cave where the porcupines lived. All of these places had left her feeling clearer and more whole, more in touch with the infinite wisdom of spirit. She had thought these priceless gifts of Nature came to her through Keith.

On top of that, he was the one person in her life who had said he wanted her, who had appeared in the doorway of the house she had reluctantly called home, when she was feeling most abandoned. In many ways, she had felt she didn't have a right to exist except through him; she had been conceived in error, and her mother would certainly have aborted her if she could. Her biological father denied her existence. Keith was the first person to recognize her value as a human being, and the first to acknowledge her abilities as a healer. Now she realized she could let go of needing that validation, knowing and trusting that spirit, brought into manifestation through Nature, is a constant companion, an infinite source of love and consolation. Spirit always offers illumination when it is required.

Pleased with this new perspective, she waited for the hunter to depart. After a few hours, she told him decisively that it was time for him to go, and he wandered away into the woods with the golden dog. Turning towards the South, facing along the beach stretching away so smoothly into the distance, she surrounded herself in a bubble, a sacred circle that no one was allowed into, except for wild creatures. Just before dusk two marsh hawks came. They were obviously mates, and they played together, swooping around her, flying high and then low to the ground, dropping out of the sky and catching themselves, swerving to and fro. When darkness fell, they disappeared into it, but at dawn they came back and stayed for the day. They were very chatty. Even later, when she faced the ocean, she could feel them behind her, and she would turn to watch their acrobatics.

She reveled in the glory of the sunset, enjoying the darkness that enveloped her. She fell asleep wrapped in her blanket, waking just before dawn to watch the sky grow purple, pink, red, orange and then gold, until finally the red ball of fire rose up through the haze. Pelicans flew by in long lines, their slow majestic flight always a delight to watch. A blue heron came and stood on its long legs in a marshy area. But her most profound visitors were two little beach bumble bees, reflections of the tattoo she'd had done on her arm a couple of months previously. She was sitting with her legs crossed and the bees nestled in the sand next to her knee, so she could see their stripes quite clearly, and even their little yellow eyes, dots without a retina. They taught her creation songs, told her how to create what she wanted in her life, and how to become one of the bee people so that she would always have them as allies. They taught her the frequencies and tones of the bee tribe so that she could become one of their family. She felt so warm and welcomed, it reminded her of the blanket wrapping ceremonies that the native people do when they adopt someone. She stroked the tattoo now on her upper arm, happy to have been so gifted.

She felt like she was being adopted by the ocean too. Yemaya can be demanding—she doesn't casually take you on as a daughter. But the elements had always agreed to protect Char as long as she honored them, and she knew how to feed them, how to give back to them, how to thank them for the regeneration they brought. Yemaya's favorite gifts were fruit and liqueurs, or something very sweet. Char usually took honey or molasses when she went to the ocean. Whenever she ate, she left a little food for spirit. It made her happy to give like that. Now she had no food with her, but she had cigarettes, and she took one out, standing up to sprinkle a little tobacco in each direction, singing her prayers. When she lay down to sleep that night, she cried, with gratitude for the deep blue/black beauty of the star studded sky surrounding her, and all the other gifts that were offered to her so freely.

On the third day, a friend came to take her home. After this time alone, she felt cloaked in light, quite removed from ordinary human concepts, and she spoke little on the way back to the city, although she laughed a lot. She had received the clarity she sought from the retreat, and she was deeply grateful.

Extracting unwanted energies is the most common kind of healing work that Char does, since energies that attach themselves to people are sometimes very toxic. They take all kinds of forms and they may be very cunning. She is always willing to do what it takes to help someone, but occasionally it requires a very concerted effort on the part of her and her power animals. The following occasion was a particularly memorable one.

Char had just finished smudging (cleaning herself, the room and her instruments with the smoke of burning sage and cedar), when her first client of the day knocked at the door.

"Come in!" she called, and someone cracked the door hesitantly. Char smiled hugely and the crack of the door broadened to allow entry. "You must be Martha, come on in, make yourself at home! Where would you like to sit, facing the window or away from the window?"

Martha was small, with short dark hair, wearing a brown and yellow jacket, which she took off and put on the arm of the sofa. A beautiful band of blue shimmered over the left side of her head, enhancing her physical beauty. She had never met Char before, and was a little nervous. "Umm...where do you normally sit?"

"I'll sit there!" Char waved at the padded blue rocking chair. "My allies tell me whatever I need to know wherever I am, but they like to stand against the window, so I can see them from that chair." She laughed. The client sat down on the sofa, smiling as she began to relax.

Char realized she had a cigarette in her hand. "Are you OK with cigarette smoke?"

The small woman nodded, "Yes, it's fine."

"Good…" She took another drag, admiring the blue smoke as it curled in the sunlight. "A friend of mine says you should never trust a psychic who doesn't smoke! It helps to keep me grounded in the physical." Laughing again, she sat down with her left leg curled under her, crushing the cigarette to death in the ashtray. Her rattle, an intricately painted gourd with a bone handle, a gift from a grateful client, lay on the table between them. Picking it up, she said, "The first thing I do before a reading is rattle, to clear all the energy, then I sing, then I call in my allies with a prayer. Does that sound OK?" Her inquiring look met with a definite nod. "OK, let's begin."

Closing her eyes, she shook the rattle above her head to the right and to the left. The sound was centering, calling her to settle into herself. The song came through, swelling out of her throat in high drawn out notes that sank away to a deeper level, and finally to silence. She never really thought about the song, it just was what it was, whatever was called forth to clear the space. This was a song that she had never heard before; sometimes it was one she knew well.

The song done, it was time to pray. As usual, the allies she called in were from a number of different traditions. "Aho, Wakantanka, Great Spirit, allies, mother, father, grandmother, grandfather, Parvati, Siva, Kali, Mother Earth, Father Sky, Great Mystery, all gods and goddesses, All that is, and All that is not, we invite you here today to assist us. Help us to bring forth only what is good, true, and beautiful. We are always grateful for your presence in our lives. May all that occurs here today be only for the highest good. Aho."

Shaking the rattle one more time, she placed it on the table between them, smiling at her client before she closed her eyes again, focusing. Immediately a form took shape behind the woman, a man standing there, pulling on something…like a piece of her skin, or a piece of her spirit, pulling on it and unraveling it: unraveling *her*. He was surrounded by darkness. Char immediately knew that he had been sent by someone.

"There is a guy, an ex-lover, his name starts with a C…he doesn't wish you well!" She laughed a little, to dispel some of the negative energy, not because it was funny. It wasn't funny. But laughter is a good way to prevent being pulled into negativity. She opened her eyes.

Martha was frowning. "I can't think of an ex-lover whose name begins with C."

"Well, he has sent something that is attached to you, and it's not very nice."

It is never easy to know what to say when you see something so malevolent on someone. Char didn't want to scare her. She tried to see something else about her, but she couldn't see past the demon. She couldn't very well say, *you have Satan standing behind you, fucking with you.* Obviously this entity had to be dealt with, and it was not necessarily going to be easy.

"Hmmm…I am getting the sense that you are not here for a reading at all," she said slowly.

Abruptly, Martha burst into tears, pulling a handkerchief out of her pocket to blow her nose. Reaching over to the side-table for a box of tissues, Char put them in front of her. In between sobs, her client told her, "I've been having this problem, this man has been following me. I'm beginning to think I'm going crazy…"

"Is it a man that only you see, or do other people see him too?"

"It's only me that sees him…I don't know if I'm imagining it, or what, but he seems so real, and I can't get rid of him. " She wiped her cheeks.

"OK…" Char nodded, this made sense. "Well, you are not imagining it, I see him too and I think he is pretty real!" She needed to find out if her client had a history of psychiatric problems, because if that was the case this might have been going on a very long time, which would make it more difficult to remedy. "Do you have any history of this kind of thing? Has this ever happened to you before?"

"No, nothing like this has ever happened to me before. I have a pretty regular kind of life, I'm in school, and it's going well, I'm doing my MFT. I should be graduating next year. I live with a good friend up near 21st Ave, we have a great apartment there, and I have a boyfriend whom I really love. Everything in my life was really fine until this started happening."

"How long has he been there?"

She hesitated, thinking. "I first noticed him…maybe four or five months ago. It's hard to say because I didn't really believe it at first, it was very gradual that I began to notice him."

"Hmmm…what made you decide to come to me?"

"I told a friend of mine in school about him, and she said *you* need to see Char. She gave me your phone number."

"Well, I think I can help!" Char laughed. "Don't worry, my power animals and I can get rid of him. I'll use the rattle around you. The rattle helps us to *re*-member who we really are and therefore *dis*-member what is not who we really are. It helps us to become more cohesive. And my power animals will come to extract him, and I may need to use a crystal to cut the cord that is holding him to you. You might feel something, you might not. Whatever you feel, that's fine. You might want to cry some more, you might find yourself laughing." Snow Leopard was already prowling around, snarling a little, and Raven was floating over her head. Char stood up with the rattle in hand, glancing around for the crystal that she used for cutting away schmutz. It was lying on the bookshelf. She leaned over to scoop it up, placing it on the table beside her. Meanwhile the entity had become more demonic.

"You can't get rid of me," it snarled, with something like a laugh, except that those kinds of entities don't know how to laugh. Its head was pulsating, growing and shrinking as it glared at Char. To avoid the demon's thrall, she was careful not to look directly at it, but out of the corners of her eyes she could clearly see its horrible roving eyes glowing in the black shadowy mass that was its face. Shivering, she felt the hairs standing up on the back of her neck, and stepped back so that she was hidden in the black feathers of Raven. She knew that her allies and animals could do the work, and she just needed to stay out of the way. She felt herself enveloped in the being of Raven, and reached out for Snow Leopard. She was right there, huge and warm. The wind of Raven's wings, gracefully powerful, made the scene in front of her shimmer.

She rattled around Martha's head and shoulders while Snow Leopard paced and Raven floated. Both moved in, the big cat twining herself between them, and the black bird flying around the demon's head, talking to him, offering him a place to go, telling him he could no longer stay here. Usually, the entities she dealt with loved her power animals, and would do whatever they asked, but this one was too evil and tenacious to be easily talked into leaving. Still, the energy of Char and her allies were more powerful than him. He started to writhe in fury as the places where he was attached were giving way. Raven was calling and clicking, as she flew around him, and Snow Leopard was growling. The demon was swearing, a series of long drawn out groaning sounds, as he strained to hold on and shake the power animals off. Char could see the anger and hatred emanating around him, swathes of dark muddy stuff. She rattled and prayed, focusing all her power on perceiving Martha without him. Rarely did an entity hold out beyond her persuasive abilities, but this one was both clever and very determined. He melted into a bird shape, distracting Raven for a moment, then she was back, offering him a healing to take him home to himself, or to someone who could help him. Char tried not to watch, concentrating on staying out of the way, bringing in only the good, the true, and the beautiful.

Then, partly in an effort to protect himself, and partly because he was unwillingly intrigued by the animals and what they offered him, he released his hold on his victim. Immediately Snow Leopard was pulling him away. He screamed and groaned, but the battle was over, only a thread left attaching him to the woman. Char groped on the table beside her for the crystal, and her fingers closed over it. In a second the thread was cut. Like a piece of elastic, it sprang away, and disappeared. Snow Leopard returned, and she and Raven pulled out the last strands that were left hanging around Martha's back and shoulders. Char flung them out of the window, and rattled some more to finish cleaning her up, closing her aura, making her whole again. When spirit was satisfied, Char sat down, relieved that it was over, appreciating the energy field in the shaft of sun that came through the window. Such a presence as that, with such evil intentions, was never fun to deal with.

Somehow a cigarette was in her hand and she was lighting it. As she drew the comforting smoke down into her lungs, she noticed the blue sky outside the window. It was a beautiful day.

"Well!" She laughed. "He's gone, I'm glad to say! He was nasty. How are you feeling?"

Martha looked very different without the man behind her, much lighter, almost shining. The blue streak Char had noticed when she first came in was intensified, and her chest had a golden glow. She was smiling and crying at the same time, twisting the handkerchief in her fingers. "That was so bizarre…I could feel something…I don't know how to describe it, I could feel him being ripped away from me…and he's gone now!" She glanced behind her, turning back to Char with a big smile.

"Yes, he's gone, and I don't think he will be back. If he does come back, let me know right away! But they don't usually return once my power animals have done the work. That's very rare."

"And you know what I just remembered, I do have an ex-lover called Chuck!"

As Martha spoke, Char could see him, a handsome guy in his early thirties, with shoulder length blonde hair. As she looked, he faded away.

"Yes! I would stay away from him if I were you! You have some old connections with him, but he doesn't have your interests at heart. Don't let me get too woo-woo on you, this life is enough to deal with, I don't want to start going on about past lives. You are done with him now, you don't need to repeat that old shit. But, you know, we all get stuck in old stuff sometimes.

He's got to get his shit together, and he needs to let go of you. You should rest for the next few days if you can, because he has been draining you for a while, and you may feel off balance. Don't try to do too much, eat properly, and drink a lot of water."

She nodded. "OK."

The voice of spirit spoke to Char again, and she repeated the words. "Spirit is telling me that you need to spend time in your garden." A happy little plant spirit, maybe a rose or a lilac, danced across her vision. "Those plant spirits like you!" They both laughed.

"Yes, I love my garden."

Char glanced at the clock. "Time's nearly up, but do you have any questions?"

"Well…I was wondering about the guy I'm presently seeing. Can you tell me anything about him and our relationship?"

Usually Char heard voices telling her what to say to her clients, but today, for some reason, there were only pictures. She saw them together; he was a little older than her, and very much in love. She saw them getting married, and having children, then some difficulties. Then, transposed over the wedding, there was another man standing off to her right, smiling at Martha. Strands of light connected the two of them. A third image presented itself, again over the other two. Martha was sitting behind a desk talking earnestly to someone: it was her career, her work. Char didn't look any further than that, there was no need to know more. She was always leery of looking far into someone's future, not wanting to influence people too much, because things can always change. The power of human will lies in the here and now, and that is its beauty.

"He's good for you, he really loves you. He'll take good care of you. There is someone else in your future, and at some point you will need to decide how you want to relate to this other person." Spirit was speaking to her now, and she repeated the words. "You won't be able to deny the bond between you, though of course you have a choice in how you act it out on physical plane." Spirit was saying, *whether you have sex with him or not*, but with this woman she figured it was better not to be so blunt. "You will meet this other person soon, though you may not immediately recognize how significant he is. Also, your work is going to be very important to you, and it may conflict at times with your family and your relationships. You have big work to do in the world," she laughed. "You are a talented artist, I see beautiful paintings—" she paused and shook her head in amazement "—oh! Soooo beautiful! Paintings and sculptures. Your art will be of great benefit to many people, it has a very healing quality. You have a tendency to think it's not important, and it would benefit you to acknowledge that it is. It's not the only work you will do, and it won't always pay the bills, but it is important, and you need to allow your inspiration to flow through you. There is an infinite source of inspiration available to you!"

Glancing at the clock again, and smiling kindly back at her client, Char picked up the rattle. "We have to wrap it up now, I have another client coming in five minutes. Are you OK?"

She was crying again, little tears rolling down her cheek. She wiped them away with a handkerchief that was now a sodden mass, and Char handed her the box of tissues. "Thank you *sooo* much, I feel so much better."

"Good! Well, let me just thank the allies for their beautiful work." She rattled to the right and to the left, and another song filled the room. This was one she knew well, one of her favorites. It felt exactly right to offer this song as a parting gift. Of course, it always *is* exactly right; that is the incredible thing about leaving everything up to spirit. When the last notes died and the room was clear and still, she rattled again, and thanked her allies, then she put the rattle down, grinning at Martha. "OK, that's it, you're all done!"

She stood up, gathering her jacket. Looking like a little child, she said, "I'm so grateful, I don't know how to tell you how grateful I am."

Char got up too, giving her a hug. "It's my pleasure, I'm glad I was able to help."

She had money in her hand. "$100, isn't it?"

"Yes, it goes on the altar over there as a gift to spirit," Char pointed out the chest where the pictures of Siva and Guru Mai sat surrounded by rose petals. She put the kettle on in the kitchen, needing another cup of coffee to refuel her after the intensity of the drama she had just been through. Martha tucked the money between two candle holders, saying, "I thought you'd prefer cash."

"It saves me going to the bank. Thank you, take care, spend time in your garden!"

Martha smiled again, wiping a tear from her cheek. As she opened the door to leave, her eyes caught Char's, and her words came from a deeply heartfelt place. "Thank you so much!"

Chapter Seven

Once psychic readings had become a regular part of Char's life, she developed a very close and easy relationship with the non-physical allies who were always there to help her. Today, spirit was calling her from the other room, saying, "Time to connect, time to connect!"

"I just have to get my coffee and take my multivitamins!" she responded from the kitchen, as she poured the coffee into her cup and the pills into her mouth. Her allies were already talking to her from the corner of the office, and she made her way in there before she realized she hadn't put sugar in her coffee. "Hold on, hold on, I'll sit and connect in just a second!"

Finally, she was relaxed and comfortable in the warmth of the office. One of her allies is a very tall man, very masculine, and the other is a very feminine woman, who has been with Char since she was seven years old, when she first saw the transparent form of the beautiful spirit in front of the fireplace. Now, standing in the corner, she just looked like a normal person, but sometimes she has wings. Those two are always there, plus a third presence that she is aware of, though she doesn't see it.

They appreciated each other and admired the brightness of the day, sharing the beauty together. Crows came to share the good morning magic as well, sitting on the branches of the cedar tree outside. They all honored the brief relaxed connection time, as she waited for them to express their readiness. Sometimes they commented about the person who was coming for the reading; they might say, "Oh, we are excited to talk with this one, we have been waiting a long time." She wondered how long was a *long time* for spirit.

The light played, and the allies shifted in constant visible invisible motion, in the space behind the red sofa, in front of the leaded glass window.

They never seemed to want to occupy any other space. There was a knock at the door, and Char opened it. A perfect connection coursed through and over her, as the two humans in physical form greeted each other with smiles. The eyes that met hers were filled with questions.

She waved her arm at the sofa, saying, "Find a place to sit, did you bring a tape?" Spirit shifted in the corner, spirit connecting with spirit, and images began: a flicker of an argument.

She spoke the prayer, calling in allies from various traditions. "Great spirit, Tankasila, creator, creatrix, all that is, all that is not, Kali, Amachi, Parvati, Ganesha, Quan Yin, Quancun, Christ, Ave Maria, power animals, allies, Oshun, Yemaya, many faces of god, I ask for only the good of the masculine and feminine allies and ancestors to be present in this reading today, I ask that I be able to get out of the way, and let the Great Mystery do the work. May there be eloquence and understanding between us, for not only us two but all our relations, for the next seven generations and all of the earth's children. Thank you for the opportunity to do this work, may I be a hollow bone, a ho, mitakoyasin."

Song came, and the images gained volition: a beautiful man offering money, an opportunity, packing boxes, an airplane, there was loving, and then an empty apartment. Images were followed by feelings, as spirit spoke in the corner. There was a child—she felt the intimacy of their exchange, then there was a train, the child was going, but she heard a voice saying, "I'll be back, I will never be away from you." She described the images. Then spirit spoke, and she repeated: "This fellow is loving you, but he seems to be loving you from a distance, is that what you want?"

She looked to the right, where spirit guided her to three specific images of her client in the past: one older teen image, one young teen image, and one child image, which explained why she was pushing this guy away, even though he was a sweet man. "It's not that he is not right for you, but you don't want him to *shock* you. There is an image of you at nine or ten, your family moved, and you were not informed about the change; so there is something about fear of shock, your brain is afraid of other people orchestrating your life without your knowledge, without consulting you. The man who loves you is a distance away now, but that can change if you want it. Realize that you are in charge of your own life now, all of your changes now are created by *you*. He wants to move closer, and the choice is up to you. He is a sweet man, and it is important that you align your desires with what is being offered to you." Spirit was talking all the time, interjecting information. "I see travel opportunities will be available to you, and spirit says it's a job, I see an image of it happening in three months. And if you desire it, there will be another partner." She saw to the left another person whom she knew was a potential lover. Her client could choose to have this partner that she was pushing away now, or she could choose to have another one. "There is an image of the desert, in the next year and a half there is a trip to the desert, and that is when he will show up. He will come from the desert. You get to choose. If you want love, show up for it! These are your options. Any questions?"

Spirit didn't give her a chance to ask questions because there was more information, an outline of a man behind her. "Oh, there is a dead guy, a friend of yours from school, and it looks like he committed suicide." She got a flash of him hanging himself, and he told Char with words that her client was a friend to him when he was feeling unloved. "I'm sorry about his death, but he seems fine now, and he wants to say that he really appreciated your friendship."

Spirit said from the corner, "Tell her the money is coming through. The judicial system is crazy but her needs will be met, she is not to worry." Char got a hit that this money situation was causing a lot of anxiety, so she asked aloud, "So then, the best way to keep her sanity in this situation would be…?"

Spirit replied, "She needs to understand that the person whom she feels is against her, is *not* against her. The situation is there to teach her. She should try to understand how alone this person feels, and see that this person wants to be understood. So the solution requires recognition of that person from her. And no sudden body movements, this person is easily startled. Be careful not to cause him alarm."

Char repeated that, and then spirit wanted to give her a mantra, so that when the woman was in court, she could repeat it to herself. The allies were arguing about what was best, the tall man wanting to use one phrase, and the beautiful woman another. Char laughed uproariously. They were soon in agreement that she should say: *It is now safe for me to transform, I am more capable and compassionate than I have ever been.*

Glancing at the clock, she saw that an hour was almost up. Song sprang from her throat again, a lilting liquid sound that healed as it floated through the room.

From her first days as a healer, Char had an aptitude for removing undesirable energies, which is a skill that has many applications. Because of her teenage experiences with drugs, she was particularly interested in working with drug addicts, removing drug entities. She understood that many of the people who retreat into using drugs do so because they are psychic, and cannot handle the psychic input that is coming at them. Meeting Loren opened up the possibility of working with that population.

Loren was a professional dominatrix with a house in Vancouver, BC. Since her services were in high demand, she had plenty of money and she used some of it to help the street kids in the city, providing them with somewhere to eat and sleep when they needed it. Always interested in alternative healing, she first got in touch with Char to have some shamanic work done on herself. Finding it deeply transformative, she asked Char to come to Vancouver to spend a few days doing extractions and soul retrieval work on some of the kids she took care of.

It was a demanding task. For three days, Char worked to remove the drug entities that were devouring these people. Some were intrigued by Char, but really had no interest in healing; they were only there because it was entertaining and free, since Loren was paying for it. Others, however, were surprisingly receptive to the work. One such person was Morgan.

Morgan was twenty, and even though her face was covered in sores from crystal meth and heroin, an astute onlooker could see her beauty shining through. She was tall and thin, with big brown eyes that stood out in her gaunt face. Although emaciated by the toll of the drugs, her body had a natural grace. Eyes like Char's could see the gray sheen that enveloped her, that would continue to eat away at her as long as she allowed it, until it had eaten the whole life out of her. She had been an addict for most of her teenage years, and if she chose not to change that, soon there would be nothing left.

She came over for dinner. Char was taking a break from doing soul retrievals, and enjoying the delicious food that Loren's maid served with soundless grace. As they sat round the table, Char talked about the work she did, how she and her power animals formed an alliance to remove the entities that had attached themselves to people, creating negative dynamics. Morgan herself was painfully shy, and said barely a word, though she was clearly interested. Noticing this, Loren asked questions of Char to draw out examples of the healing work.

At the end of the meal, Loren turned to Morgan and said, "So, would you like a soul retrieval? I'll pay for it. But obviously it's your decision."

Morgan chewed at her lower lip. "Would it...would you be able to help me?"

Char met the anxious gaze with her usual relaxed assurance. "If you are ready to be helped, then my power animals and I will do what we can."

"Does it mean I'll give up drugs?"

"Perhaps, if that's what you want. It depends why you're taking them and how much you want to give them up." Her blue eyes, always filled with laughter and yet shining with truth, met the young woman's brown eyes, communicating silently her desire to help, and her awareness of the goodness of life, which made her so trustworthy.

In spite of the fact that she had only just met Char, the sense of unmitigated joyful loving that she exuded touched Morgan deeply. She felt

Char's presence both as commanding and yet soothing. She had been taking drugs because she could not deal with the psychic images that she constantly received from the world around her (not that she used the label *psychic*, she just thought she was crazy), yet here was a person who had learned not only how to deal with them, but how to put them to good use. Although she was afraid that, without the drugs to insulate her from reality, she would be overwhelmed by a feeling of her own worthlessness, she was ready to take the risk of giving up her addiction, with the prospect of Char's and Loren's aid.

She sighed. "OK, I'll do whatever it takes."

Char smiled broadly. "Cool! So let's do it tomorrow, how does that sound?"

They made an appointment for the next day. Morgan's gray sheen made Char aware that she did not have long to live, but she knew that would change if Morgan consciously chose life, and she always believed that whatever was for the highest good would prevail. Working through her power animals, she extracted the entities of the addictive drugs, which she saw as fast moving, evil grinning, demonic little creatures living smugly inside Morgan's body. During the process, Morgan consciously paid attention to the images that she had previously worked so hard to avoid. She saw the crystal meth as a skinny little girl who walked around to everyone in the room, whispering her messages of wishfulness and warning: "You'll feel so much better if you take me!" "I'll make you happy!" "Don't try to be around all these people without me, I'll make you feel comfortable!" She didn't see Char's power animals, but she saw the skinny girl fall silent and then circle, so that she was standing with her back to Morgan, looking at something Morgan couldn't see. Finally she walked away and disappeared.

The heroin entity was very tall, and looked a little like death. Morgan saw herself standing dwarfed before it, between its feet. Its long tapered tail curled around behind Morgan, and entered her guts, entwining itself into her. As Char pulled it out, she felt a shudder through her body, followed by an unfamiliar sense of emptiness in her abdomen.

The following day, Char returned to Seattle, to her normal work routine. Some of Loren's proteges managed to kick their addiction after the shamanic work, and one of those was Morgan, who was having a hard time, but sticking to her decision to stay off the drugs. Rather than go back to sleeping on the beach with her druggie friends, she stayed at Loren's house. Every day, Loren made sure she got up, did a few odd jobs, and ate three square meals. They talked about various options Morgan could choose to help her rebuild her life. Although she was from Seattle originally, and wanted to go back there, she was afraid she would just get into drugs again, since that was all she knew. Would her connection to Char extend to something more than the work they had just done together? Loren believed in Morgan enough that she agreed to call Char, suggesting that Morgan be an apprentice.

When Char first heard the suggestion on the phone machine, she shook her head in doubt. She was living in a house in Greenlake with two other people, and they had just been ripped off by a couple of drug addicts they had befriended. She didn't want to go through that again. But when she asked spirit what to do, they were very clear that Morgan should come and stay there. So she shrugged and agreed, accepting that spirit knew best.

With a small reservoir of cash from Loren, Morgan arrived within the week. She found her way to Char's house, a single story blue building set in a large yard in a rural area. Cautiously—which was her mode of being in all things since rejecting the drugs that buoyed her up with false confidence—she approached the door. A note was pinned to it, with her name written in large letters. She took it down.

"Hallo, Morgan! I'm glad you're here, I'll be back about six. The door's unlocked. Please come in and make yourself at home, help yourself to whatever you need in the kitchen, it's straight ahead when you enter. The TV is in the bedroom to your left. See you soon! Enjoy!"

It was signed with an exuberant scrawl that offered Morgan a vividly heart-warming picture of the wild laughing woman who had saved her life.

She stayed with Char for six months, making her home in a small trailer at the back of the house. The three adults who already lived there made her feel welcome and loved. Owing to her shyness, her presence was very non-intrusive, and she also turned out to be as honest and trustworthy as any of the three residents could have wished. In return for room and board, she worked at the store that Char owned at the time, Serendipity, taking care of customers when Char was in the back doing readings. Although still very wary and nervous, she was keen to learn, and listened well, so the people who came in to chat, particularly those who supplied the gemstones, books, cards, incense, herbs, and other items, found a ready ear. Morgan had grown up in the Mormon Church, and she found these peoples' radically different view of the world much more in line with her personal experience of spirits as entities present in her immediate environment.

She joined in one of Char's classes, which met one evening a week in the store. Sitting on a cushion on the floor, with four other women, she listened avidly as Char told them about the aspects of the major Arcana of the Tarot. It was an excellent tool for Morgan learn about herself, and she loved it. One by one, each week, they worked their way through the archetypes. Char could draw people out, reaching each of her students on a level they could relate to, so that it was experiential for each of them, going much deeper than a mental exercise. Fed by Char's unjudgmental acceptance, Morgan's self-esteem grew, and she used the tools that she was learning about—her own psychic abilities, as well as animal, plant and stone totems—to improve her life. Within a few months, she got herself a job as a sales clerk at Safeway. At the end of six months she had begun to make her own friends, and she moved out of the little trailer into her own apartment. By the time I met her, some four years later, she had a steady job and a steady relationship with a fine young man.

She remained close friends with her mentor, and Char was as delighted as Morgan herself, to see her walking through the door of joy.

As Char became well known, people started asking her to work abroad. One of the places she went was London. While she really enjoyed the excitement and stimulation of visiting new places, she said, with a slight shudder, that she found London very difficult—everything was so old, and so clogged with spirits that were stuck. She stayed in a hotel that was choc-a-bloc with beings clamoring for her attention. The air in the room was milky, almost opaque, particularly as she was going to sleep, when it was really thick with spirit, full of tangible memories.

She couldn't pretend she wasn't aware of them. She talked with those who would listen, explaining that they were dead, and they would be better off in the Land of the Dead. "It's OK to be dead, you know, you don't have to continue doing all these same old things that no longer serve you, waiting for someone to see you and acknowledge you," she told them. Although they understood her on some level, they were lost in a kind of limbo, knowing they wanted something else but not knowing how to find it. She made a deal with them: if they would leave her alone for the week she was there, she would help them before she departed.

One of the spirits, a woman, seemed to be in charge of everything. Char saw that although she had no established partner, she was deeply loved by someone. Later, she found out the hotel bar was named after the mistress of a ship's captain, who spent a great deal of time there. She assumed that this was the woman who seemed to be so in her element. Unlike the other dead people, she wanted to stay, and since she wasn't troubling anyone, Char didn't try to persuade her otherwise. There was also a cat that no one else could see, that often sat on top of a clock on the TV. Char thought of it as *the cat on the blinking time*. It was a Siamese, its little tail and ears the color of coffee. It would flash across the room, playfully jumping and pouncing on unseen things. Char had the sense that it was really the woman, shape shifting.

The building was right on the Thames. In the past that was still so present, Char saw boats, and nets, and rats running everywhere. The dead beings included sailors, soldiers, chambermaids, fishermen, prostitutes, a handsome merchant, a pickpocket, a couple of gentlemen, two well dressed ladies, and a ragged young urchin with a mischievous smile. Some of the ghosts had been there for centuries, some only a hundred years or less. One of the gentlemen had died in a duel, and one of the chambermaids in childbirth. A few had drowned, and several had died in fights, but sickness was the main killer. It no longer mattered, how they had died, although some of them were still stuck in the tragedy of their deaths; they all had stories they wanted to tell. Char saw the threads of life that these dead people were attached to as opalescent, shimmering, and white; life still beautiful, just as it is in the present, even though it was past.

At the end of the week, she fulfilled her agreement. Sitting in a chair, she rattled, and her power animals came to do the work. Seventeen dead people were hanging out, waiting and ready to go. Since they were on a busy river and that's what they were familiar with, boats were immediately available to take them. Four people got on the boats really quickly, but the others weren't so easy. Some wanted a power animal, and one being in particular was adamant about being reunited with a family member. It was a lot of concentrated work, negotiating with many different entities until everyone was satisfied. When the last ghost had finally left, she gave her power animals a gift, and thanked them, pleased with a job well done, but grateful that she was going home to a city less riddled with the past.

Another place that Char visited was France, where she went with Claudia, to celebrate her friend's fiftieth birthday. She was enchanted by Paris, and had one of the most wonderful experiences of her life at Sacre Coeur. Walking along, looking at the rows of statues, she heard someone quietly calling her: "Pssst! Psst! Come over here!"

She looked all around to see who it was, until she finally accepted that the voice came from the last statue, which was of Jesus. *Uh oh*, she thought, *I've lost my loop, is there a microphone in there, or what?* She could clearly hear him saying, "Come over here!" She went over and knelt down.

Once she was settled, the voice said, "I am not your guru but I would really like it if you would just listen for a little bit."

"OK," she said, deciding that she might as well go along with it. She could accept there was some entity inside this statue. He was very handsome, with a beard and shoulder length hair, and the feeling that emanated from him was deeply benevolent. The sweetness of his presence made her want to listen.

What he had to say was nevertheless unexpected. "Do you think this is a fun job for me?"

"I dunno," replied Char, a little taken aback, and unsure how to respond.

"This isn't fun, you know, I am not having a good time here," he told her.

She felt his weariness, understanding that people don't relate to him. They maintain their distance from him so that they can keep him on a pedestal, separate from themselves, and then use his name in rituals that he doesn't even like. His desire to talk to her was based on seeing her as a human who knew herself.

"Now close your eyes," instructed the statue. She did so, and immediately there was movement, then she was off on a wonderful shamanic journey. He was showing her that god is in everything, everything is sacred, everything is *that*, there is nothing that isn't *that*. Soon she was in tears with the intensity of the beauty she was seeing, perceiving things like a brown leather wallet, a lighter, a plastic bag, a glass of juice—all of these mundane things that no one would normally describe as godstuff—as the most incredible, astounding artifacts, possessed of beauty beyond anything she had ever been able to imagine. She saw Nature and things from Nature in a way she had never seen them before. It was glorious. She heard the voice again telling her, "All of this is god." And she felt the god-ness of it all, understanding that everything that exists is permeated with that god-ness.

Char was hesitant to tell me about this experience, because she herself is cynical about people who claim that Christ speaks to them. "I don't want to pretend that I channel Christ!" she said. "I mean, is He really that available to be channeled? I don't think so! But what he showed me was so profound. It really opened my eyes, it changed my life. Whatever that archetype was, it had Christ energy, and I'll always be deeply grateful for what it shared with me."

Chapter Eight

Christianity was not one of Char's favorite religions, but every now and then, she found a church with a method of worship that suited her. The Baptist Church on 5th Ave always had interesting ministers, with radical and open minded viewpoints. Char initially went because Claudia asked her, then she enjoyed it so much that she kept on going. Barb, Claudia's sister, also went regularly. One Sunday after the sermon, Char was chatting with Barb when a distinguished-looking gray-haired woman came up. Barb greeted her with a hug. "Margaret, how nice to see you!" She turned to Char. "Have you two met? Char, this is Margaret."

The stranger shook hands. Char tried to concentrate on her but was distracted by a very handsome young man looming behind the woman's shoulder. He was saying, "This is my sister, I need to talk to her, tell her I need to talk with her!" He was a very bright shining being, with very benevolent energy. He obviously wasn't going to shut up until Char acknowledged him, so without speaking aloud, she assured him that she would pass the message on later, when it was appropriate, and would he please leave her alone for the moment. He faded away a little, staying close by. Char chatted with Barb and Margaret about the service, and shortly Margaret said, "Well, I must be on my way, I have to pick up the boys. It was nice to meet you, Char!" She smiled radiantly and departed.

The young man remained, hovering at the corner of Char's vision. She turned to Barb. "I have to go home too, but I need to ask you something first." She glanced around and took Barb's arm, casually leading her out of earshot of the crowd. "Does Margaret have a deceased brother?"

Barb's eyes flew open in surprise. "Yes, indeed she does! In fact, that's how we know each other, Ben and I were lovers. He was drowned about thirteen years ago, when he was twenty-four. They never found a body, but we have assumed he's dead."

The young man came into the center of Char's vision, clearly ready to bombard her with information about how he died. "Well, he's telling me he wants to talk with Margaret," she said, downplaying his eagerness in case his desire wasn't reciprocated. "Would you give Margaret my phone number and tell her to contact me if she wants to talk to him?" She raised her eyebrows questioningly.

"Of course! I'd be happy to do that. I'm sure she will want to hear from him!"

"OK, well, let her know!" They said goodbye, and Char went to her car. The young man followed her, and muttering quietly, she told him, "You can leave now, if Margaret calls me, then you come back, OK?"

He politely departed.

Ben's disappearance had always been surrounded in mystery. Because he'd been into drugs, he'd developed some friends who were not the most savory characters. Knowing that he owed money when he died, some people believed he'd faked his death to escape payment. The official version, undisputed by the police, is that he fell overboard on a yachting trip with some friends, and drowned. But inconsistent stories from his so-called friends, and apparent pre-arrangements around how they were informed of his death, led the family to believe he might have been murdered. Their search for clues had been fruitless.

Margaret was immediately interested when she heard that he had asked Char to be a go-between. She called Char to set up an appointment, asking if it was OK for her sister, her mother, and Barb to be present. After a quick consultation with Ben, Char agreed.

They met in the house where Ben and his sisters had grown up, where his mother still lived, although now estranged from Ben's father. It was a beautiful huge A-frame building, with a lovely well-kept wooded area around it. Char walked up the concrete path, aware of Ben eagerly awaiting the opportunity to talk with the people he had loved so much when he was alive. Masses of flourishing greenery met her, treetops towering over the roof of the house, thick hedges insulating her from the street. This was Capitol Hill, one of the busiest areas of Seattle, though you would never know that. Dusk was just beginning to fall, and the evening scents of healthy growing plants made her smile with joy. She rang the unimposing doorbell, thinking, "These people have created something wonderful with their money."

A white-haired woman, with a clearly sweet and loving aura, appeared in the doorway, and smiled a welcome, which Char returned with all her usual openheartedness.

"You must be Char," said Kay, holding the door open for her.

Char stepped inside, saying, "Yes, I am, and you must be Ben's mother!" She was immediately struck by the similarity in their features.

"It's very kind of you to come," said Kay, as they shook hands.

"Oh, it's a pleasure! You can thank Ben, he is the one who brought me here!" Char laughed, as she followed Kay into the big open living room, with a high ceiling reaching up into the top of the A-frame, where the walls met. A wood fire glowed red and orange in the metal, pyramid shaped fireplace set against the narrow vertical wall. Three women stood to greet her: Dorothy, the older sister, Margaret, the younger sister, and Barb. Char swept them with a smile, thinking how beautiful they all were. A sense of expectant excitement hung around them. Barb gave her a heartfelt hug, and the other two shook hands. Char had already warmed to Margaret, whose soft kindness matched her mother's, but Dorothy was a little stand-offish. Char hoped she would become more accepting as time passed.

Although large, the house was friendly and inviting. Comfortable armchairs were arranged by the fireplace. "Will you be OK sitting here?" asked Kay, indicating the central chair. "I don't know what kind of lighting you need."

"Oh, don't worry, this is great! I don't need any special lighting, he will come through however!" She glanced around the big room and shook her head in awe. "This house is gorgeous!"

She made herself comfortable in the center, legs tucked under her on the cushioned chair, her audience sitting around her in respectful anticipation. She explained the process. The young man was waiting impatiently, golden light swirling, hovering around them as they sat. She could tell that Margaret was his favorite sister, although he loved them all.

She said a prayer, and sang, interrupting once to laugh as she addressed the air, "OK, OK, let me finish singing!"

The song ended on a long low note, and she immediately leaned forward with her eyes half closed. "Well, Ben is right here, and he is very keen to talk with you!" She chuckled. "He says he has been wanting to connect with you for a while. He says to tell you he is fine, and very happy, and he has been watching your lives and helping you when he can. He loves you all very much. He's very glad you are all here. He really wants to talk!" She laughed, and paused. Because he was a very benevolent spirit, with only the best intentions, and no hidden agendas, she allowed his energy to merge with hers, until she could feel his being inside and all around her. She sat up a little straighter, and the onlookers saw some subtle change occur in her facial expression and tone of voice. Margaret, observing with a hint of skepticism and a great deal of excited interest, felt a change in the atmosphere, too far outside the physical to be labeled, yet very distinct. Char turned, speaking directly to Kay, who was sitting to her left at the end of the sofa. Her manner and tone were gentle, almost fatherly, but she seemed to be having a little trouble breathing.

"He says you were a wonderful mother to him. You are not to grieve for him...he's still with you, he's never been away, he's around this house a lot. He's sorry his disappearance...his death caused you so much pain." Char's breath came in gasps as she spoke the words, "I love you, Mother."

She paused, inhaled deeply a couple of times, and began to speak slowly, with frequent pauses. "He's telling me how he died, he seems to think you will all want to know that. He says...I owed some money to someone, it was drug money. That man was on the boat. He gave me a drug which affected my judgment, slowed me down physically, preventing me from resisting. I didn't know what the drug was when I took it, I would take anything anyone gave me at that point. The man was a friend, I owed him some money, he was very upset with me. He hit me and then pushed me overboard on the west side of the boat. In that state I couldn't swim." She bent her head.

There was a long pause, and Dorothy asked, "Did you know you were dying?"

Char took a couple of shallow breaths, and said falteringly, "I knew I was drowning...I couldn't help myself...I felt rage...and terror...and anguish." Her voice broke, and her breath seemed ragged. There was a short silence, and she shifted in her seat, then got up, visibly shaking.

"Are you OK?" asked Margaret, who had been watching her closely, seeing her distress.

"Yes..." She moved towards the sliding glass doors, trying to calm her rapid breathing. "I'm sorry, I just need to go out for a minute and smoke a cigarette. It's not usually like this..."

She slid the door open and stepped out, gulping lungsful of the cold fresh air. The porch light spread its diffuse glow into the darkness. She lit her cigarette as she wandered over to a big tree with huge low leafy branches. Ben was showing her sweet things to soothe her, telling her how he used to love playing here when he was a child, and she began to relax again as she felt the joy he had experienced here. The agony of not being able to prevent himself drowning faded from her awareness, and she wiped away the tears that had been sliding down her cheeks. He had not intended to upset her. He was such a bright angelic presence, a lovely being, slim and tall, with beautiful curly hair and huge soulful eyes.

When she went back in, they were standing around anxiously, and she reassured them with her ready laugh. "It's very rare that I feel someone's death like that, usually it's easy for me to keep my distance, to know that whatever

I'm seeing, it isn't about me," she told them. "I guess he is such a sweet spirit, I let him in closer than I usually do! He has a lot of very powerful energy. He's very strong, very intense. I felt him grasping my hand, and that made me shake with his energy."

They settled down again, but before Char began, Dorothy asked, "Who was the man who pushed him overboard?"

Char replied directly. "It really doesn't matter who killed me. You knew him. He is dead now. There is nothing you can do. Let go of blame and judgment. You are wasting your time. I was on a slippery slope, I didn't love myself…I killed myself, in a way, and it's a good thing I am dead. It was awful and frightening at the time but it's for the best, and now I am largely at peace."

"We won't go after anyone, we just want to know who it was," Dorothy insisted.

"It was a dark haired man, and he was living in Chelan." Char spoke as though she was seeing the murderer. "But Ben is saying, 'I don't believe you, you need to let it go and get on with your own life.'"

"Well, can we find his body?"

"He's telling me it isn't where they said it was." She paused, laughing a little. "There are a lot of bodies on the bottom of the lake but mine is not one of them. The boat wasn't on the west side of the lake, it was on the east, and anyway, they took my body out of the water after I died." She cocked her head on one side to listen to what she was being told. It seemed bizarre to her, but she repeated it anyway, with interjections as she *saw* what she was being told. "The men on the boat started worrying about how they might get into trouble, so they got some diving equipment and collected my body. They took it to shore in a small motorboat and put it in the back of a truck—it was a brown truck with a canopy—covered it with plastic, and took it to an apartment in the city. A very nice apartment…one of the owners was called Tony…and someone else. Then they drove the body down to Renton." She paused, listening. "Yes, Renton…then they took it to a house east of the mountains. I'm seeing a sign…" she hesitated. "It's the name on the mailbox. I can't see clearly what it says, some Polish name, or Eastern European… ends with *wicz*. The owner of the house is called…Jay…no, James. It's a white house, a little way away from the other houses on the street…there's a root cellar, they buried his body there. I'm getting the sense that they moved his body again from there, or they're going to move it…Ben says you will find his body eventually, there's no need to send out a search party, it *will* be found, before Mother dies. But it doesn't matter anyway. You are to *let it go*!" The last words were spoken with great emphasis, although accompanied by laughter.

She spoke then to each of them, one by one. Her tone reflected exactly the different interactions he had once had in physical form with the different members of his family. With his mother, there was a deep loving gratitude that permeated the room, making Char very emotional, crying and gasping. "You loved me so much. I can't love you enough from where you are." He was watchful and protective, wanting to repay her for the way she had taken care of him. "I have tried to guide you from this place but I haven't always been able to. I will be here, on this side, when you come. No one was here for me when I died, I was in a kind of no-man's land because I died so unexpectedly. There was no preparation. I will show you around when you come."

Then Char spoke from her own perspective. "He wants me to give you a pendulum. It's a gift from him, not from me. I can see what it is, it's at my house. I'll give it to you later."

With Margaret, his younger sister, there was a teasing but deeply affectionate quality, which felt to Margaret exactly how they had related when he was alive. The last of her skepticism dropped away as she listened, and she was deeply delighted to feel her brother's presence. Again, Char became emotional and had a little difficulty with her breathing. "I love you, Margaret, because you are so smart! I wish I could get close to you again. I feel a huge love for you." She saw a little boy, with a striking family resemblance. "Oh, he loves his nephew, he hangs out with him often, and he is thrilled that he is named after him. He says, 'I am his godfather, and I take that as a serious responsibility.'"

Margaret laughed. "Yes, little Ben asks about you often. But I'm concerned that he is obsessed with the ugly aspects of your death."

"I won't talk to him about that any more. I'm a guide for him, I give him his creative self. He should pursue some movement arts, make sure you offer him that."

"What about his brother, Conrad?"

"I'm not so interested in Conrad. He has a different guide, a woman."

"Is it someone I would know?"

"He says, 'Yes, it's Mamie, for crying out loud!'" Char laughed uproariously at Ben's impatience, and they all joined in her lightheartedness.

With Dorothy, his older sister, there was a very slight authoritative hint to the tone, and Margaret smiled, remembering how Dorothy and Ben had always had a competitive edge with each other. "You need to get on with your own life and let go of what happened to me. You are wasting your time, stop trying to blame someone for my death. You have many talents, and I have been working in the background with you over the years, helping you. Now accept that I am gone, and be willing to relate to me on the level of someone who has left the physical world behind. I have been coming to you in dreams, and other times, bringing you messages to help you in your life."

Dorothy nodded. "Yes, I've had some vivid dreams of you."

"I've pushed you the most. Pay attention to my messages, you need to fulfill your potential. You hide your feelings to protect others, be more expressive. Write about your feelings. Tell the truth about your emotional life. Live in a more soulful way. You have a wonderful, blessed life. Take advantage of the opportunities that present themselves. A young woman, pregnant or with a small child, will ask you to undertake something soon, and it will seem like a burden, but you are to do it. It will honor your youthfulness."

Barb, with whom he had once shared an intensely passionate relationship, was now married to another man. Ben was very loving, while still making it clear that he had a real desire to release her. "I want you to fully love your husband. He is a better man than I could ever have been for you. I had no strong male role model. Bless the relationship you are in. And there will be another child."

He referred to several of his old friends and relatives, sometimes with sound advice and other times simply with a greeting. "Give Buddy a slap on the back from me!" He told them he had Christmas gifts for them all, so they needed to pay attention, to make sure they didn't miss anything.

They all had questions, and he patiently answered them as well as he could. But there was one taboo area. "I won't answer questions about our father, you can ask about anything else." As she said these words, Char saw how he had felt himself to be a failure in his father's eyes, and how he had blamed his father for causing his mother unhappiness.

"What did you learn from being alive?" asked his mother.

"I learned that it is about loving people when you have the chance, and it's about keeping commitments. Don't make promises you can't keep. I am very ashamed of my involvement with drugs. That prevented me from taking care of myself."

"Is there anything you need from us where you are?"

"I love food, put food outside for me sometimes. Take care of the garden, I love to be there. I miss the old chestnut that was cut down. Keep on having the yearly gatherings for me, I love them. I want to meet and talk with you all again."

"Is there anything I could have done to make your life better?" This was Dorothy's question.

"You could not have done anything. I wish I had had more male support."

"What's it like for you, being dead?"

"At first I wasn't interested in evolving, I wanted to stay close to human life for a while. It's hard to describe, hard to find words. It's a feeling, a connection to what people call god. God is everything, and when you die you become one with that. Now I know I am as beautiful as anything."

"Are you going to be re-born in this world?"

"Yes, as Margaret's grandchild! But I have twenty or so more years, by your judgment of time, here in this afterlife, learning and evolving."

He had one last request for them. "I want you to hold a *burning*. Burn some food for me, and give away gifts to each other. That will help me to let go. I feel a deep soul connection with you all, I love you all very much."

It had been a long session. When they were finally done, and Char came back into the present physical realm, they all expressed their deep gratitude for the opportunity to talk with Ben again, an experience none of them could even have hoped for.

"Everything you have said about his death is consistent with rumors we heard, and also with what was said by another psychic we went to," Kay told her with a gentle smile.

When she left, Margaret escorted her to the door. "Should I talk to our father about this?" she asked.

Ben had made it clear he could not forgive him yet, so Char shook her head. "No, let it go. There's nothing you could say that would make any difference in this life."

Margaret nodded reluctantly. "OK, I'll let it go. On a different note, I'd like to come and have a private session with you sometime. I'll call you."

Six months later, Char gave another reading to the family. Ben told them then that he was reaching peace with his father. He said he was now able to come through more easily in dreams, and he felt a sense of completion, which would make further meetings with Char unnecessary. Addressing his mother directly, he said, "I want to move forward toward spirit, to move to a different plateau, and spend less time with human forms. I need your permission to go on to this next level." Of course, Kay readily gave her consent.

Margaret came for readings every six months. At first Ben was always present, offering advice, but after a couple of years, when his sister asked after him, Char told her, "He's happy, very busy. He says he's sorry he doesn't have a lot of time to relate to you on this realm any more. He's moving on to other realms. He's telling me—"she laughed "—it's hard for him to put it into language you would understand, but he says, 'I have earned my wings.' They are not literally wings but it is the closest thing I can say that you might understand."

Once a month, Char does work for donation only, which usually means free. It often ends up being more than once a month, because Char hates to turn down people in need, knowing that her gifts can help them—and they also know that. It's her contribution for people who don't have access to a lot of money, which is something she knows about. This particular morning she got up at 8:30 to do a pipe for a woman whose baby had just died. Char is not a morning person, and 8:30 is too early for her—she often works until 10:00PM—but this was the only spare slot she had.

There was a knock at the door and Char, drinking her coffee in the kitchen as she swilled down some vitamins, called "Come in!" Martin entered, his long hair as straggly and untidy as ever, nervousness oozing all around him. He was the drug addict who had once lived upstairs. Smart enough to know a good thing when he saw it, he had kept in touch with Char, frequently bringing her various other down-and-outs who needed help. The woman whose baby had just died was one of his finds.

Char welcomed him with her normal warmth. "Hallo, sweetie, how are you? I'm just making my coffee!"

"Good morning, how are you? I'm fine. Eloise isn't here yet?" His voice was slightly clipped and uncertain. It didn't carry with the confidence of Char's, as though he felt himself to be ugly, in contrast to Char's consistent awareness of the presence of beauty. In spite of that, he was friendly.

"No, what time did she say she would arrive?"

He turned away, muttered something inaudible, and then turned back to say, "I brought some feathers for a give-away."

"Oh, Martin, that's great! How sweet!"

They sat down to look at what he had brought, which was a sizeable collection of feathers from many different birds, when there was another knock at the door. This time it was Eloise and her guy. They were both very silent and hesitant, only half present, sunk in a chasm of grief. *Perhaps a little drugged too*, thought Char, as she greeted them with her habitual sweetness.

Everyone sat in a circle on the floor, and Char put the pipe, wrapped in red leather as always, in front of her. She unwrapped it slowly, removing each piece with care and love. She took a long pipe cleaner and poked it through the stem until she was satisfied. "I always clean it after I have smoked it, but then it always wants me to check it whenever I pull it out again!" she laughed. Picking up a plastic bag of herbs, she said, "Now this is a mix from my Dad of some herbs especially for grief. I don't know exactly what's in it, but he used to be very good with herbs and he made up several special mixes. Before we start, the pipe has reminded me to ask, did you bring something that belonged to the baby?"

The sad-eyed woman produced a tiny pair of socks, and Char instructed her gently to put them on the piece of leather that lay in the center of their circle. "We are going to make a bundle to honor the baby before we finish, and it needs to have at least one thing that belonged to the baby in it, so if you have anything else you want to go into it, then put it in the center too. Is that OK?" The woman nodded blankly. Char laughed a little. "Good! Normally we would put in a piece of his hair but I understand you don't have any, so that's fine, we can use the socks. You will keep the bundle for a year and then dismantle it and give a part of it to each direction. OK? If you need help with that you can call me at the time, but I think the pieces will tell you what wants to happen to them."

She turned her attention back to the pipe, filling the bowl with the mixture from the bag. Then she paused, laughing again, and turned to the woman to say, "Well, he is talking to me already! It's so funny, because he appears to me as an old man and I keep having to remember that you know him as a baby! He is telling me that he really knows how much you loved him and he really appreciates that. He says this dying thing—" she laughed "—that's what he is calling it! This dying thing was an arrangement between you and him before you came into this life, and he wants you to know that, because although he knows it is really hard for you right now, he says it is all for the good in the long run, and he is very happy where he is now. He says the reason he died is because you need to understand compassion. He says you have known compassion as a sort of mental thing but now you will know it as something you yourself have felt and you will learn to have compassion for all kinds of other people." She paused and frowned, biting her lip and looking a little anxiously at the woman, who remained quite expressionless. "I hope that is OK to say, it seems a little harsh?"

The woman's eyebrows raised and she gave some semblance of a smile. "It's fine," she said, speaking so quietly that Char had to lean forward to catch her words. "I want to hear whatever he has to say."

The pipe was ready now. "OK, first you should know that what you pray for when we smoke the chanupa *does* happen! So be careful what you pray for! I call the pipe the 1-800 line direct to god, because that's always how it has been for me." The sound of her laughter filled the apartment with warmth. "Now, I am going to smoke the pipe and say a prayer and I am going to pass it to you first, Eloise. You will smoke it and say your prayer, and then pass it on to Peter. He will smoke it, pray, and pass it to Martin, and Martin will do the same and pass it to me. We will keep going round until it is all finished. When you pass it, you hold the bowl in your right hand and turn it like this, so that the person receiving it will be offered the stem first." She turned the pipe in a circle. Eloise looked confused, and Char laughed. Both her voice and her laughter had deeply sweet and loving tones to them. "It doesn't matter if you don't get that right, it'll still work! You don't have to say your prayer out loud if you don't want, the smoke will carry it up to spirit anyhow. When you draw on the pipe, don't inhale, the smoke is for the Creator. If you need to re-light it, there are matches right here." She pointed to a box on the floor. When Eloise nodded her confirmation, Char put the pipe to her lips, sucking deeply as she applied a flame to the bowl. The flame inverted and clouds of blue smoke poured out from Char's mouth.

"Aho, Great Spirit, thank you for the honor of doing this ritual, and for the honor of holding the chanupa. May all that occurs in this circle be for the highest good. I pray for this child who has just died, that he may have an easy passage, and find the joy that is his. I pray for Eloise and Peter, that they may find the peace they need, and that the lessons they need to learn may easily be integrated, and that the compassion and comfort they need in this time of hardship will be easily available to them." The bowl was glowing now. She took the stem in her mouth again, more smoke spiraled up to spirit, and she said a few more sentences before she passed it on. Deep in their grief, both Eloise and Peter completely lacked the kind of luster that Char portrayed. They said their prayers silently, and did not draw hard. When the pipe got to Martin, it was out, and Char held the flame to it while he sucked. Since he had smoked a pipe with Char before, he was easier with it, so he spoke his prayer aloud, wishing in his still tentative voice that the bereaved couple might find what they needed.

It was Char's turn again, so she poked at the contents of the bowl with a dead match, relit it and prayed some more. The pipe went round one more time and then it was dead. She emptied it out onto a small piece of red cloth that lay in front of her, tying the edges of the cloth together with string.

"These ashes will be part of the bundle," she explained. "Does anyone else have anything to say?"

Martin nodded nervously. "I just want to say, Eloise, that you don't need to grieve because he hasn't really gone. He's still around, you just can't see him."

Char was wrapping the pipe, respectfully placing each piece in its correct place within the red leather. "Well, Martin, you need to allow them to have their grief process. It's true that the baby hasn't gone anywhere in a spirit sense, but this is a physical world we live in, and we are physical beings, and he is no longer here physically so that is a loss. It is a great loss, and she is going to experience it that way. She needs to be allowed to experience her grief so that she can get whatever it is she needs to get from it. If she stifles her grief, then it will just sit there forever."

She turned to Eloise. "We need to make four prayer ties for him, to go in the bundle." Taking some more small pieces of red material and some pinches of tobacco, she showed Eloise and Peter how to make the ties. Fumbling awkwardly, they spent several minutes tying up the little squares of cloth, while Char sat by, radiating soft calming energy. When they were done, she put them on the leather in the center of the circle. Then she looked at the couple questioningly. "Is there anything else you want to put in the bundle?"

Eloise shook her head, but Peter prodded her, muttering something, and she said, "Oh yes, wait!" with the first sign of animation she had shown all morning. She fished in her back pocket, bringing out a tiny blue bonnet. "This was his." She placed it on the piece of leather. Char nodded, smiling, and reached forward, using both hands to lift the hide closer to her, with everything lying on it. She sprinkled some sage, followed by a pinch of tobacco, on top of the open bundle. Then she carefully folded it up, with all the items inside. She tied each end with leather ties and put one across the middle, handing it to Eloise when she was done.

"This hide is deerskin, and the deer is about gentleness, so you will have some gentleness while you are going through this grief. You are to organize a feast and do a giveaway for people who knew the baby. Then put the bundle on an altar and feed it regularly, with food that the baby loved, then in a year from today, open the bundle and release the baby's soul to each of the directions. Is that clear?" She looked at the woman kindly but searchingly, making sure she understood.

Eloise nodded expressionlessly, and Char reached out to touch her knee, with a warm smile. "OK, then I guess we are finished. It has been an honor to do this, thank you!"

Char works with people from every walk of life. Eloise and Peter are at one end of the spectrum, while Damion and Maria are at the other. They are influential in the music business, and very well heeled. One day, Char came home to a phone message from them. "This house we've had built on the beach at Orcas Island is finally done, and we want you to come and do a house blessing here, and then we're going to give a party and we want you to do readings. You've helped us so much, we want all our friends to have the same opportunity. We'll fly you out here, we have a private seaplane, and we'll put you up in a local hotel. Whadd'ya' think? Give us a call and let us know how much you would charge for the day. You'll love it out here. The whales swim by in pods."

It was an offer she couldn't refuse. She loved flying even in a big plane—closer to god was always how she thought of it—and the small plane delighted her. The work began with the house blessing: even a new house has all the energy from the emotions of the people who built it, and from the people who lived on the land before. Damion had invited the architect, who was very wrapped up in his own world, needing to be acknowledged as the most important person around. His inner struggles were blended with other uninvited stray energies she expelled.

An unquestioned assumption of beauty pervaded the relaxed atmosphere. The men were casually elegant, wearing expensive but unobtrusive clothes, the women impeccably made-up, in beautiful dresses. There were thirty five people at the party, and Char did fifteen readings. People mostly came in couples. Before she began, Damion said, "There is one person I want you to meet, so when you are almost done, let me know, and I will send him to you for your last reading. That'll be my silver bullet!"

The first couple came in a little nervously. Char quickly put them at ease with her relaxed charm, as she shook their hands and sat down.

"OK, first, I will say a quick prayer, and then I sing a song, then I'll start talking, and there will be a short time for you to ask questions at the end, OK?"

They nodded, and she launched into the prayer. Spirits were talking to her already, and as soon as the song was done, she repeated what they were saying.

"Spirit is telling me that you, Jonathon"—she nodded at the young man—"are at a crisis in your work situation, you've been offered a job abroad and it's very well paid, but you don't want to move. You don't want to be away from Beth, and she doesn't want to go with you." Jonathon and his wife glanced at each other in surprise that Char would pick up this so quickly. She carried on, offering him options and telling him what might occur, depending on his choices. Then she turned to Beth, smiling in delight as she did so. "Spirit is showing me pictures of a beautiful baby, it's a little girl, oh, she's so beautiful! And she's yours, or she's going to be yours, she's a being you have had past lives with, and she's waiting to be born." She paused, listening, furrowing her brow. "OK, spirit is telling me you want to get pregnant, but you've been having trouble, is that how you've experienced it?" She stopped for confirmation, and the woman, already tearing up, nodded mutely. "OK, they are telling me that you have an unresolved issue with your own mother, and you won't be able to conceive until that's been dealt with, because you are afraid you will repeat the mistakes your mother made with you. They're saying that you don't actually have to resolve it *with* her, although you could do that, but you need to believe in yourself, you need to know that you are not going to do what your mother did. You are a different person, and you don't have to do what she did."

Char paused, checking that her audience understood. She repeated it in slightly different words, offering a couple of possible solutions. "You could do some mediation with your mother, but it's not essential, you are not dependent on her in order to find a peaceful resolution within yourself. A good therapist might help you, though. Once you've done that, once you're at peace about it, you'll be able to get pregnant. And you're going to have a wonderful little baby girl!" She clapped her hands with joy.

Only half an hour had passed, but Char seldom did a reading without touching people's hearts, and the kinds of truth she spoke, in such an authentic fashion, broke through most people's barriers. Beth, like many others, left in tears, saying, "Oh, Char, you are so good!"

Seeing her ruined makeup, Char thought, *I certainly haven't done your mascara any good!*

A few of the people she read were not so happy with her abilities. When she looked at one woman who had come with her husband, she saw another man in her present and her future. He was so clearly there that Char couldn't pretend she didn't see him. She said to the woman, "Oh, you are interested in someone else!"

Immediately the woman stood up to go, saying, "OK, thank you very much!"

"No, wait, spirit isn't finished, we have to sing!" said Char, her eyes wide. The woman sat down again for the song, then left as fast as she could, her husband trailing behind her.

Char worked until she was exhausted. It was dark when she finally came down the broad stairway, admiring the beautiful unmarred decor. Her employer, smiling, offered her a glass of wine. "So are you ready for my silver bullet?"

Her face fell. "Oh Damion, I'd forgotten about your silver bullet! I don't think I have the energy for anyone else!"

He raised his eyebrows in exaggerated disappointment. "I have to have my silver bullet! I promise you won't regret it!"

She followed him towards a side room, and he introduced her to Maria's uncle, a small brown smiling man, who bowed over her hand. He was Filipino, with an amazingly gentle but powerful presence. He was indeed well worth waiting to meet, and Char delighted in reading for him. One of his guides was a woman with wings. When Char mentioned her, he smiled, saying, "Oh yes, she comes to me as a bird." It was a very easy reading, mostly done in silence, because there was no need to verbalize what was being communicated.

Chapter Nine

After Char asked me to write this book, I assisted her in some of her work. On my way to my first house blessing with her, I searched all round the car, unable to find the map that gave us directions. Annoyed, I muttered, "I suppose I'll have to stop and call."

Char smiled. "That's OK, this kind of thing happens often on the way to soul retrievals and house blessings. The spirits know they are going to have to move on, so they're trying to prevent us getting there. They're tricky!"

I agreed, as I spied a phone booth, and pulled up on a deserted street. We both got out. While I dialed a friend to give me the instructions I needed, Char lay on the empty sidewalk with her hands behind her head. When I was done, we walked back to the car, which was round the corner, and I noticed she seemed to be talking to someone who was invisible to me.

"Who's that?" I asked.

"Just a street bum. I think he died here, and he's lonely," she explained.

"What does he look like?"

Char cocked her head on one side, a little surprised at my question. "Just like a street bum!"

"Well...how do you know he's dead? Does he look the same as he would if he was alive?"

She considered this for a moment, and then said, "Well...yes, he does look the same. I just know he's dead."

"You can talk to a spirit that is alive, just like you talk to a spirit that is dead, right?"

"Yes, and I just know when they are dead." She paused, thinking. "Sometimes I may not be sure, but then I ask, and they tell me."

I unlocked the car door for her, and she got in. As she was closing the door, she addressed the space: "No, you can't!" She slammed the door quite fast, turning to me a little apologetically. "He wanted to come with us, and I had to tell him that would be no!"

We arrived at the house only ten minutes late. When we rang the doorbell, Hannah's small frame appeared in the doorway. She introduced us to Bill, who was taller and more reticent, though also very friendly. It was cold enough for us to need coats outside, and every time Char came back in from smoking a cigarette, Bill would remove her coat for her, hanging it neatly on the coat rack.

Hannah told us about the house.

"We bought it three years ago. Before that, it was a doctor's office for many years, so I think maybe it has picked up a lot of stuff from that time. Strange things happen here, but the oddest thing is how hard it is to heat. Somehow, no matter how much we stoke up the stove, the heat never gets to the back rooms. We had someone come and install a gas heater, it was an expensive and very reliable kind, but it just wouldn't run. The guy said there was nothing wrong with it. He kept coming back and trying to make it work, and finally after he had been here about ten times, it seemed to work. But even when it was on, it didn't seem to put out much heat. And the front of the house, which is rented out, has had a gas heater for a while, but it also won't stay lit. The woman who works there said she was watching the pilot flame one day, and it was fluttering just as though someone was blowing it, although there was no draft at all in the room, and then finally it just went out."

"It's not just the heating problem, strange things happen here," added Bill. "One time I left a backpack sitting on a chair in the back room, and then it was missing for three days. On the fourth day, I found it sitting right there on the chair. But I know it wasn't there in the meantime, because I'd been looking everywhere! Stuff like that is just really annoying."

Char, sitting on a stool by the stove with one leg tucked under her, leaned forward, putting her notebook on the table. She nodded slowly. "Well, I do think it's very haunted. Anyway we'll see what we can do. When are you expecting your allies to turn up?"

"This sounds like them now," said Hannah, and she went to the door. Sure enough, two people, a man and a woman, were just coming round the corner. They introduced us, and pretty soon we were all sitting in a circle, with a makeshift altar—four candles and a crystal on a white cloth—in the center. Char instructed Bill to light the candles, and picked up her rattle to begin calling the directions. She had only just started rattling around her head when she stopped, opened her eyes, and said to Hannah and Bill, "Does one of you have a dead relative you are attached to?"

Bill responded immediately. "Yes, I do."

"And you want to have her around?" The question was asked without any judgment or assumption.

"Yes."

Char nodded. "What's her name?"

"Kathleen."

"OK." Again Char closed her eyes, shook the rattle over the left side of her head and began to call in the East.

When the directions had all been called in and Char had asked that only the good, true, and the beautiful be present for this house blessing, she put down her rattle and stood up. The others remained sitting; their job was to hold the ground. My pen poised over a notepad so that I could take notes, I followed Char into the front room. She stood in the doorway for a moment, eyes closed, then stepped forward, muttering under her breath. She brushed her hand across an armchair that sat to one side, saying, just loud enough for me to hear, "There is someone sitting here." She looked around, then began to clap her hands vigorously in one corner, all across one wall. Moving around the room slowly, she paused at one point to have a muttered conversation.

The next room was more difficult. She had a long conversation with an entity that apparently stood by the window.

"Yes, I understand that," she said, "But now you have to go." Pause. "Well, where would you like to go? To the Land of the Dead?" Pause. "My allies will escort you there." Pause. "They will give you a healing if you like." Another pause, then Char smiled. "Good!" To me, she muttered tersely, "A young man who loved hunting."

She turned away, looked in the corner, spoke under her breath, and made a graceful motion with her arms that I understood to mean she was getting rid of some unwanted energy. We moved across the hallway. Clapping all across one wall, she said to me over her shoulder, "Someone overdosed here…didn't die, I don't think…but very afraid." She stared at the corner for a long time, with her head first on one side and then on the other. "Hmmm…kids… there seem to have been a lot of kids here. They don't mind moving on." She moved her hand in a circle, and went slowly out of the door into the bathroom. I stood in the doorway while she had a long, only half-audible conversation with someone. She turned to me. "Someone died in here." She turned away as though to leave and then suddenly turned back. Her Raven spoke its caw, raucous in the silence. She shook her head sadly, saying, "A lot of disappointment in here, like they were expecting some healing they didn't get." I stepped back to let her past and we went on to the central room where everyone else sat silently, except for Bill, who was standing up looking very uncomfortable. Char paid no attention to any of the physical beings. She walked around the room slowly, pausing to remove some energy from a painting on the wall. Then she moved on to the second bathroom, and again I stood in the doorway. She looked at the bath and said quite clearly, in a tone of surprise, "Oh, look at you! What are you doing there?"

I laughed out loud, and out of the corner of my eye I saw one of the human allies laughing too. As Char moved closer to the bath, I heard her say, still in a very friendly tone, "I'm so glad you like it, but you know you can't stay here any more!" She spoke over her shoulder to me, "She says she really likes the new bath." A brief pause. "There are all kinds of places you could go, would like to go to the Land of the Dead?" Another pause. "Well, you *are* dead! My allies will take you there and give you a healing." Pause. "Good!" She turned away from the bath, glanced around, and spoke to the corner in a less amicable tone. "You need to leave, you are not welcome any more." She waved her arms in a circle, throwing whatever it was out of the window, as she grimaced at me. "I don't know what that was, but I didn't like it!"

Walking past the wood stove, she looked at the floor, then turned in a circle and laughed. "There's a little dog running around shooing the ghosts out! Oh, that's so sweet! I've never seen anything like that, it's just this little black dog!"

An entity in the kitchen drew her attention next. "I really don't think this is the right place for you." Pause. "Yes, I know, but that's no way to talk to people!" Then she backed out of the kitchen, raising one hand almost defensively. "All *right*, all *right*!"

Our next stop was the bedroom. I heard her make an exasperated sound. "No, you can't stay here!" Pause. "Oh no, no, no!" She shook her head, laughing derisively. "No, I don't believe you! You really have to go!" She glanced at me and rolled her eyes, saying in a low tone, "There are three of these guys, and they're really tricky, I don't know how Bill manages to sleep in here." She continued her conversation with them, and finally turned away, looking satisfied. Standing in front of the bed, she sang a few notes in her beautiful clear voice, brushing her hand over the bedclothes.

Now we were done. Back in the main room, she picked up the drum. "Is everyone all right?" she asked, addressing the visible human beings who sat around. They all nodded. "OK, Mikaya and I are going to walk around and seal off the area. It won't take us long."

We returned to the first room, and she drummed around its perimeter, stopping once to remove something unseen to my eyes. The second room was similar. In the third room, however, she stood for a while turning around in the center, and then said to me, "This room needs some mirrors."

In the bathroom she passed one hand across the wall and then hesitated for several seconds. Finally, she said, "You agreed to go, you can't come back." There was a pause, she nodded with satisfaction, and drummed rapidly all around the walls.

The kitchen again held her attention for a few minutes. After listening and muttering, she shrugged and said, "OK, if you insist!" She drummed, and passed on to the bedroom, where she put the drum down to have a brief non-verbal argument with something in the corner, until it exited through the window, aided by the dance of her hands.

At last we went back to the central room, and she beamed around at everyone. "OK, now we get to eat! How are you all doing? You did a great job holding ground! What about you, Bill?"

He was kneeling and leaning against the wall, but now he got up with the others. "Well, I was really uncomfortable in my body for a while there, but now I feel better. I don't know what was going on, I just had to get up and move around."

Char nodded as though she understood, and then one of the others claimed her attention. Hannah bustled around getting food together, and soon we were eating delicious pesto seaweed rolls and miso soup, served with crackers and goat cheese. Char was outside smoking by then. Sometimes when she is working, she fails to eat properly. She isn't one of those psychics who sits in a chair and goes into trance, leaving her body; I have seen how she burns up energy as she works, the sweat literally pouring off her brow. I reckon she is quite thin enough, and her body needs all the sustenance it can get. So I disturbed her smoking session to bring her in to eat.

While we were munching, Char had me read off my notes so she could tell Bill and Hannah what had gone on. She explained that in the first room, her Raven had pulled out some sadness from the corner. "There were drugs hidden somewhere, I felt kind of dizzy, couldn't get a grip on anything, and then I had an image of an elephant, I think it was the Hindu god Ganesha, sucking out the drug energy. I also saw lines of communication all over the place in that first room, filling up the whole space, and they had nothing to do with you guys, so they needed to be connected to whatever had been using them, and sent away from here. Then there was a woman sitting watching, so an angelic presence came and took her. She needed to be psychopomped, and she wanted an angelic presence, that was all she would go for! She also needed some self-love, so my power animals gave her the seed of self-love, and she ate it. That was pretty cool!" She laughed with delight at the memory, and we all laughed with her. Try as I would, I could not imagine what it was she saw. The paradox of my experience made me laugh. I referred to my notes:

the black pen was reassuringly clear on the white paper, though it told me of things that made no sense to my rational mind.

"You said something about an overdose."

"Oh yes, that was a guy who was lying on the floor, I don't know if he died or not. Then there was a woman who was crying, she was very lonely and sad. Hummingbirds came and she swallowed one, it was the weirdest thing I ever saw!" Her unrestrained laugher resounded around the room. "She needed their joy inside of her, and then they lifted her up and carried her off. Oh, and then a unicycle came for the dead woman in the doorway, she was looking for a way of getting to the Land of the Dead and that's what worked for her! Then there was a guy who hunted when he was alive. He was very controlling, he said to me, 'What are *you* doing here?' in a really demanding tone, like I was a little child, or something. My allies took him to the Land of the Dead. There was a really beautiful being on the bridge between that realm and this one, and that being took the gun out of his hands and dropped it back to Earth! I hadn't seen that before."

She stopped and looked at me expectantly, waiting for more prodding.

"You were clapping all over the floor in that third room."

"Oh yes, that was so weird because what they wanted was for me to come over and heal the other house—I saw this face looking at me, and I started to talk to it, and then I said, wait a minute, you're not in this house! A lot of the houses around here are really haunted. So they put up mirrors to reflect their energy back to them. Then there was a nun with a bird on her shoulder, it was a trip, and all these children who were somehow attached to her. They were happy to move on. A canoe came for someone in that room. There was a lot of emotional pain. And then the bathroom…people were going to the bathroom to hide. Some little kid had a negative experience in the little bathroom off the passageway, and a part of him was still there, like a soul part, and White Buffalo came. The kid, who is an adult now, of course, was having therapy or doing a soul retrieval or something so that he could get it back. Then there was an entity or an energy that wanted to be powerful so we gave it power, but it was to be contained until it had learned proper use of it. The allies came and put it in a learning place. There was a lot of illness showing up in that bathroom, a lot of activity. There was a tendency to say 'I am not well,' where there needs to be a tendency to say 'I am well,' so that the place radiates inspiration, instead of sickness. This house was loaded, I couldn't believe how loaded it was." She shook her head in disbelief.

"There were these weird little entities in the hallway, I don't know what they were. I think they represented fear or sadness—we cleansed them away. Then the woman in the bathtub; it had moved since she died, and she had found it again and was really happy. She wanted my power animal. That can't happen, of course, but we found her a raven just like mine.

"There was a lot of medical stuff. I saw someone—I suppose it was the doctor—he was getting so into the way the body worked, and then he suffered lots of disappointment because it didn't always work the way he thought it should. Bear came, and took him. Then there was a spirit along this wall—" she pointed to the wall in front of her "—who needed to be held and loved, needed compassion."

"How can you hold and love a spirit?" Hannah asked.

"They can be held and loved by another spirit or entity, or by someone who can see them, or a lot of times they need a mother energy to come and get them. They died needing that kind of thing, they have mother issues." Char looked at her questioningly to see if she understood and when Hannah nodded, she continued with her story.

"Then a sweet little black dog came to help round up all the demons. It was wonderful!"

Everyone laughed, and Hannah exclaimed, "Jessie came!" She explained that Jessie was a dog who had lived here with her, and died a few years previously.

Char nodded, smiling. "It was a mind creeper, going worry worry worry worry, a little worrier! It was very helpful, it rounded everything up.

"Then there was some weird religious stuff on the far side of that room. Someone who was very paranoid, who didn't feel like she had the right to exist, had made an altar there. It needed a raindrop of faith to dissolve that energy. But there was terror, and violence, in the form of little mice-like animals. A moth came and took the paranoid person. The violence was events, not memories, and it was like a fingerprint on the house, energy that was left behind. But it wasn't hard to move it along.

"Someone in the bedroom was suffering from the mentality of not-enough, and there was a lot of grief. Earth energy was needed to heal that, and my allies asked me to blow seeds of plenty to fill the space."

"Also in the bedroom you were negotiating with something tricky," I reminded her.

"Oh yes!" She rolled her eyes, and laughed. "I hate that! There were three adolescent spirits, playful in a not-good way. They were a pain. True poltergeists are really rare, but I do meet entities that have that teenage quality. They're like young poltergeists, too young to do a bunch of damage but powerful enough to cause some trouble and mischief. They were just floating around, and there were three of them, I thought that was kind of interesting. But we got them to leave.

"Then there was a praying mantis in the bed, or a cricket like thing. It was the song of this being, who was in the bed, who needed healing. It was happy to move along. In the bedroom there was a post with lots of little viperous guys attached to it, and my allies were pulling the post up, so they could get rid of the whole lot at once. Also there were horses helping me, if there were any shadows left they would get on the horses, and the horses would take them away."

Bill reached behind him and flipped through a pile of his paintings that were leaning against the wall. He showed us a picture he was working on, of a herd of horses galloping across a plain. Char laughed with pleasure. "Well, they were doing the work!" she said.

I asked her about the bit where she was talking to someone in the kitchen, saying, "It looked like you were allowing that entity to stay there?"

Char shook her head blankly as though she had no memory of such a thing, and I dropped it. She smiled radiantly around the room, saying, "Does anyone have anything to share?"

One of the human allies, who knew Char from a reading he'd had with her, said, "I could see shadows from the corner of my eye, like smoke drifting out, and now it is clear."

The other ally said she had really enjoyed herself. "The energy made me laugh and laugh, it was really funny. Seemed like a lot of work for you, though!"

Char nodded in agreement. "Yes, there were one or two things that were pretty stuck! OK, let's finish up here. If the gentlemen would break off pieces of cedar, and pin them above all doors and windows, that's the job for the masculine. And the women can deal with the floating flowers, that's the job for the feminine."

The two men took the branches of cedar that had been provided and started breaking off small pieces. The bowls of water, each with a floating candle, were waiting on the side table and Char directed Hannah to go outside to pick flowers from the garden, where primulas were sprouting profusely. "Always better to use what is growing, however beautiful these are!" she laughed, sniffing the red roses that stood in a vase. When Hannah came in with a handful of petals, we distributed them among the bowls, then we lit the candles and placed one bowl in each room, choosing a location that was visible from outside the room. We gathered again, with the men, in our circle around the altar, where Char addressed us with her usual loving smile.

"I think I got rid of everything. There have been a lot of entities living here. I hope you will find it different now. Does anyone else have anything to share?"

She glanced around, and Hannah said, "When I was thinking about this beforehand, it came to me that you might meet some of the Indians who lived here, and then I thought, no, there wouldn't be any of the Indian people here, because this used to be marshland, before white people came and drained it. But while I was sitting here holding ground for you I had several images of the Indian people and I realized, of course this would have been their hunting ground. I was wondering if you came across anything from that time? They were ruthlessly slaughtered around this area."

Char nodded. "I didn't meet any of the original Indian people but it doesn't mean they are not around, it just means I didn't meet them. They weren't right here. Actually, there were a couple of Native American people who were helpers but it felt like all the ones that were stuck were Caucasian."

As no one had any more to say, we closed the circle. Hannah wanted a reading then, and I found myself exhausted, so I slept in the car for an hour until Char was done. She climbed in the passenger door, sitting back with a sigh of completion. We grinned at each other.

"Home now?" I asked.

"Yes, let's go home! I'm getting a massage, hurray!" She grinned like a little kid, scrinching up her eyes.

We set off, stopping only for her to buy cigarettes. As she got back in with six packets in hand, I asked, "Hey Char, y'know that entity in the kitchen? I figured that you didn't want to talk about it in front of them, but can you tell me about it now?"

"Oh, you were right about that, I did let her stay there. It was his mother, Kathleen. She kept saying, 'Look at this kitchen, it's such a mess!' I told her they are entitled to keep the kitchen in whatever shape they want, and she needs to leave them alone. She wouldn't listen. But Bill wants her around, so there you go!"

Char teaches year-long classes, starting every spring, and all of those classes involve a retreat that includes a sweat. We arranged that she would come to the land where I lived, to lead a sweat, as part of my research. It was my job to build the sweat lodge. The weather was particularly cold, and I had to work in the snow to get it finished, since that was the only day that Char could take off from her busy schedule. I dragged pieces of carpet down from my garden (where they had been preventing the weeds from growing) to cover the crude structure I had erected by our old concrete swimming pool. Several times during this arduous process (the snow made the carpet much heavier) I wished that Char was coming in daylight, so that she could instruct me in the proper method of building it. I wasn't sure what tradition Char follows when it comes to sweats, and even if I did know, I would probably be none the wiser on how to build it. I set it facing approximately south, since that simply happened to be the easiest way to do it. I didn't build any altar, because I wasn't sure how to do so, or where to put it. As I heaved the carpet on top of the sheet of plastic I had already placed over the arrangement of curved branches, it dawned on me that I had better remove the six inches of snow that had built up inside the structure, because otherwise it would be very unpleasant to sit on. I crawled inside, using my hands to scoop the snow outside.

I lit the fire early in the afternoon, thinking it would take a long time to warm up in this weather. Char, Myrna and Sky were not due to arrive till five, and I was sure they would be at least an hour late, since none of them have much ability to relate to physical time. To my astonishment, their car drew up at only five thirty. I was waiting in the darkness by the now roaring fire. The bright whiteness reflected by the snow enabled us to see without flashlights. I met them in the driveway, hugged them all, and led them over to the fire. They all had stories of snow on the road, and rocks—or stone people, as Char called them—that they had brought for the sweat, although it was too late to put them in the fire. I was plying Char with questions. She laughed in her usual devil-may-care fashion, but I was aware of the importance of this ritual and knew that she would have some strict ideas about it.

"First of all, I assume you would like to go up to Maggie's house to recover from your drive, and then come back down to do the sweat when you are ready? Maggie is expecting you."

"No, we'll do the sweat right away." She sounded decisive about this, and I was grateful for her clarity. "I'm so happy to see you have everything moving and grooving! I always love to see a sweat fire. Just the seeing of it somehow warms me." She stood by the fire, holding out her hands to catch its heat, as she instructed me. "We need to have an altar between the fire-pit and the sweat-lodge." She took the flashlight from my hand to shine it on the spot. "Sky, why don't you get a shovel and mound a little earth right here? Then we need a forked stick that will be embedded in the altar and a container that we can hang from it that will hold the sage. And we need some cedar that we can use to bless the rocks with. Who is going to be the fire-keeper?"

I was making lists of what we needed in my head, but I interrupted the process to say, "I will be the fire-keeper unless Robin feels well enough, she's been sick. She's coming up here in a little while. I could come inside even if I have to be the fire-keeper." In this cold weather, the intense heat of the sweat seemed quite inviting.

"Hmmm…" I saw the outline of Char's face, her brow slightly furrowed. I could tell she didn't like this option. "Someone must be outside tending the fire," she said. "But I would like you to come into the sweat. Hmmm...oh well, we'll see if Robin turns up, I have a feeling she will."

Char is usually right. I searched around for the drinking water, and passed it to her. I had been drinking as much as I could all day, in preparation for sweating. She took a gulp from the jar and handed it to Myrna.

"Do we have a bucket for water that we can take in the sweat, and something to scoop the water out with, to put it on the stones?"

I showed her what I had and she nodded in the darkness. "Good! Now, Barbara Means Adams taught me that in traditional sweats, a woman covers her upper and lower body. I usually wear a shirt and a skirt or shorts. Everyone needs to have something to wear."

"OK. Char, I was considering putting some rocks in the sweat before we go in, to warm it up."

"I don't think so!" She thought this was very amusing, and soon she had me laughing too.

I shrugged. "Oh well, we will just be cold!"

"How many rocks do you have in the fire? "

"Twenty-one. But I think some of them will split."

"Hmmm...that's OK. We need six for the first round and then five for each round afterwards, so that will just do. I normally do four rounds."

Repeating the list in my head like a mantra, I went off to get the things she asked for, stopping briefly to tell Maggie and Vika to come on down. When I returned, my arms full of goodies, Robin had arrived, and Char had arranged that she would be the fire-keeper, provided I came out at the end of each round to help her with the stones, since she didn't feel strong enough to transfer them from the fire-pit to the sweat by herself. Sky had built a little mound of earth for the altar. I inserted a forked stick into it, hanging a can from the stick, with some sage inside. Soon everyone was present. In between our banter, Char made herself heard and we all fell silent.

"OK, now, just so you all know, no one gets out during a round, you have to wait for the end of a round if you want to get out, and once you get out, you can't come back in. But there's no kudos attached to staying in for all rounds. If you need to get out because it's too hot, or for any other reason, then that's fine, that's just what you do. Mikaya is an exception, she is going to get out at the end of each round to help Robin with the stones, and then she will come back in. Always enter the lodge going to the left, and as you go in, touch your forehead to the ground and say 'All my relations,' or 'Ho Mitakuye Oyasin.' OK? OK, let's get ready!"

We all bravely and a little reluctantly pulled off our layers of warm clothes until we stood shivering in our skimpy sweat clothes and bare feet. I put my clothes well away from the sweat, thinking I might have trouble finding them in the dark, but wanting them out of the way. Other people left their clothes close by. Char instructed everyone on the order of entry and she went in first, touching her forehead to the ground before she scooted to the left and then all the way around until she was ensconced by the door. When everyone else had disappeared after her, I handed in the bucket of water and the scoop, then picked through the thick glowing ashes with my long-handled fork to find a red hot stone. Most of them were already split, and I made a mental note that I must find better firestones for the future. One by one, I held them outside the door, where Robin brushed them with cedar. I placed them inside and Char used a pair of antlers to lift them into the pit. I counted off aloud, and when I had deposited the sixth one for Char to deal with, I thrust the tines of the fork into the ground on my left, to leave it standing upright. Feeling some resistance to the fork, I picked it up, to find that it had speared a knee length rubber boot which had been left lying too close.

Robin and I, who were the only witnesses to this, burst out laughing and then tried to stifle our giggles out of respect for the seriousness of the occasion—this was supposed to be a sacred sweat, after all. I crouched on my hands and knees and crawled inside, touching my head to the ground as I said the words, "Ho Mitakuye Oyasin." I both felt and saw a blur of Sky next to me as I sat down on the cold towel that awaited my butt, and pulled my knees up to my chest. When Robin let the door blanket drop, we were enclosed in perfect darkness, the atmosphere not yet warm enough for the rocks to hold their glow. I heard Char dipping into the pail of water, then a sizzle as she poured it on the rocks. I was very grateful for the steam on my face, since the rest of my body was freezing, particularly my toes.

Char began. "Aho, Powers of the East! New beginnings! We honor the Eagle and our one-ness with spirit. Show us where spirit can work in our lives, where we can feel spirit. We give thanks for our youthfulness, for the gifts of vision that come to us through the sunrise. We ask for your blessing on this sacred sweat. May it be just what we all need right now."

She carried on speaking and I lost myself in the rhythmic incantation, swaying my head slightly to the sound. Finally, she wound up her prayer. "So now let's each pray for whatever it is we need in order to initiate new beginnings and move on in our lives. Mikaya?"

Following tradition, we were going clockwise, so I was next in the circle. I talked for a few minutes about what I wanted to help me move on in my life, areas where I felt I had been stuck, places of old grief that needed shifting. Each of us spoke in turn, following Char's lead, and listening respectfully to each other. When it got back to her, she started a wordless song and we all joined in. Finally our voices faded into silence, and Char called out to Robin, "OK, open the door!" The blanket was pulled up and faint white light from the snow flooded in. I crawled to my left past several knees and feet, so I could get out to bring in more rocks.

The second round was a little hotter and I could feel the ticklish sweat pouring down my face, although my butt and toes were still complaining. It was an odd sensation, to be too hot at one end of my body and too cold at another. Char called in the South, asking each of us to pray and honor that part of ourselves that is childlike and innocent. What can we do to nurture that part of ourselves? We went round, we sang a song, and when the door opened again, Myrna exited in front of me—she had a recently broken arm which was causing her considerable pain, so she would stay out. I brought in more stones, and Char poured on the water. I was beginning to want to avoid the steam as it rose to sting my skin, though my toes were still appreciating the heat. Now it was the West, and Char called sweetly to Bear, then asked each of us to say what aspects of our ancestral lineage we were choosing not to repeat, but to carry forward differently. Then she had each of us go round a second time to offer gratitude to our ancestors for the qualities they have passed on to us.

In the last round, the rocks finally maintained a glow in the central pit. Celebrating the North, Char called to the Grandmothers, and one by one we talked about how we are learning to love with wisdom. Now my face was really hot and I was especially grateful for the song at the end when I was allowed to open my throat and let sound come out—there was something about making sound that released the heat from my body. At last the door was thrown open and we all exited, one by one. Standing out in the cold was initially a relief, and we were all high. Everyone roared with laughter when Maggie held up her speared boot.

Pretty soon we had our clothes back on and we made our way up the hill, leaving the red coals to die away on their own. At last we were at Maggie's, where wonderful vegetarian dishes were laid out on the table.

"Oh yes, food food food! Oh, this looks *so* good!" Char is endlessly appreciative of the simple things in life. Of course she was in demand as always, but I managed to corner her while other people were serving themselves.

"So, Char," I asked, "Should I rebuild the lodge facing east?"

She was sitting on the floor by the wood stove, her plate of food in front of her, her legs curled up under her. One of the cats had already discovered she was good for cuddles and was busy demanding them. Stroking the furry body with one hand, Char leaned forward with an intent look, pushing her wild and still-damp hair off her forehead with the other hand, as she considered my question. "Well, really that's up to you. I've never done a south-facing lodge before, and you know that as long as it's facing south, you will get a lot of coyote medicine!" I groaned, and we both laughed, then she told me, "Coyote medicine might be good for you! Do what feels right to you, though you definitely need to have an altar between the lodge and the fire-pit. You know, for me, it was fun to do it from a place of authenticity where there just weren't a lot of rules. On the land where I do most of my retreats, they have two lodges, one facing west, and that is more the warrior type of energy, it's very masculine; and the other facing east, that is more feminine. Traditionally, it would face east, but we're not doing a traditional Lakota lodge anyway. You might find it goes more smoothly if you have it facing east, without the coyote medicine. Coyote can really mess with things!" She laughed uproariously at what coyote might do.

"How do you decide what to do in a sweat?" I asked. "It seems like quite a lot of your work is connected to Angeles Arrien's teachings."

"I blend everything I have learned. Part of it I do from my Dad's teachings, part of it I do from Angeles Arrien's teachings, part of it I do from Sun Bear and Barbara Means Adams, part of it I do just from my personal relationship with the directions. Mostly it is just the latter; what I know of them tells me what is the right thing to say. It's as though I am talking to a friend, and I'm asking a friend for help."

She paused to fill her mouth with food, and her brow furrowed. "My god, this is delicious! Who made this?"

Maggie claimed credit with a smile, and when Char had finished complimenting her, she turned back to me.

"I work with the directions as my friends, I see an image of Bear in the West, and I talk to it until it nods its head, then I go to the North and I ask the circle of Grandmothers to show up. I feel them showing up, and I see an image of my Grandmother's eyes, and I wait for their nod, and that means they sufficiently understand what it is I am asking them for. I do each direction until I get a nod, and that means they are clear about the help that I need."

She took another mouthful, and I asked, "Do the directions tell you what to say in a sweat? Are you talking to them inside your head?"

"I just know what to do. In the sweat I am praying for whatever the people need to hear, so I am asking for assistance: what do these people need for healing? I am talking to the directions in my head, I am talking to them with my spirit and my heart, so that everything that I do there will involve what is for the highest good of these people. I am extending myself for that, and I don't exist, it is just the allies showing up. Each corner of the universe will be saying, this is what is needed, this particular energy is what is needed. If there are a lot of women in the wheel who are having mother issues, one direction might say they need to sing while thinking about what it means to be a mother, and then what it means to be a daughter. Every time I have done a sweat it has been very different, depending on who is there."

"Sounds a little like it's one of those occasions when you just have to get out of the way, and let it happen?"

"Yes, it's like the pipe. I don't do the pipe for me. I'll ask the pipe if it wants to be brought out for a particular person, and it will usually say, you can do this as long as you are extending it for someone else, as long as you just love this person. That is one of the reasons I don't spend a lot of time judging people, because it really takes away from the love. So just like that, when I am in a wheel, I pray that I can simply allow whatever healing is needed to come through me.

"But a sweat is not just for cleansing. Being in a sweat is like going back into the womb. You are really inside the Mother, and you don't just want to leave your toxins, and say, 'thank you, babe.' You know what I mean? There is a wonder-fulness about it and I, at least, want to leave something good even if everyone else just detoxes, which is what people often think a sweat is for. So I have to be really conscious of what is going on, to make sure there is something positive brought in, besides just letting go of the negative."

I nodded thoughtfully, thinking it is one of Char's gifts, that she leaves a positive atmosphere behind her wherever she goes, not just in a sweat lodge. Spontaneous joy bubbles up through her physical presence, spreading infectiously to the people around her. She is a powerful antidote to any negativity.

Chapter Ten

The blurb on soul retrieval was sitting on one of Char's altars (or *was* it an altar? I never could be quite sure, she had small tables and shelves all around her apartment with candles and statues, or pictures of saintly, goddess-like figures, along with a few feathers and bones and crystals). It read thus:

Char Sundust

Char Sundust is a shamanic practitioner of mixed Native American and European ancestry. She started her training at the age of fourteen with a Cheyenne teacher, Koheehut, and went on to study with Barbara Means Adams, a Lakota author and story teller. She then spent two years in a shamanic apprenticeship with Sheila Belanger, who taught her soul retrieval work. Medicine work has been the focus of Char's life since she was sixteen, and she has done psychic readings since she was twenty. She is also a shamanic artist.

Why choose to have a soul retrieval? Perhaps you have been in therapy and haven't been able to shift old stuff. Soul retrieval works well with therapy and Char often works in tandem with therapists. Perhaps you have never been in therapy, but you just feel that something is not right with you. People frequently feel that they are not whole, and it may be that they have lost part of themselves through trauma, or through the often difficult process of growing up. Soul retrievals can be very effective in dealing with old thought patterns inherited from our ancestors—often the slowest and hardest things to change.

Soul retrieval can be a very intense experience, though the full extent of it may not be integrated for several months. People who have sustained a lot of trauma—such as the effects of alcoholism, child abuse, brutality—may want to have several throughout their lives, but others find one or two are enough. Sometimes the effect of a soul retrieval is very profound; it is the kind of healing that can shift things overnight. It may also take the form of subtle shifts over time.

Preparation: After you have made a decision to have a soul retrieval, you may experience any of the following: vivid dreams, out of place occurrences, resurfacing of old memories, atypical behaviors, etc. Please keep a record of such instances for review with Char before the soul retrieval. List personal events you feel that might have caused soul loss (that is, trauma or losses). What ages were you during these events? What is your intent for this soul retrieval? Is there anything else you want to discuss before the retrieval? This information is helpful to the journey.

You may want to invite a friend to be with you as an ally during the soul retrieval. They sit next to you during the journey as your support ally. You can also bring personal items that you want blessed during the retrieval.

The Journey: During your soul retrieval, Char will journey with her power animals into other realms where she will do at least one of the following four things:

1. Find and bring back to you various soul parts that were lost or stolen in the past, and are now ready to return. A soul part may depart from you of its own accord due to some trauma, or there may have been people in your life who took parts of you, perhaps because of their own wounding. In the latter case, Char and her power animals will offer a healing to the individual who took the parts, in order to get them back. When the soul retrieval is over (when the drumming stops) Char will blow the soul parts into you through the top of your head, and into your heart.

2. If you want, her power animals can do extractions—removing any undesirable energy that is clinging onto you, as a result of unresolved issues from your past, social conditioning, traumas, armoring, ancestral beliefs, other people or entities trying to control you. Extraction work alone can be very profound.

3. She may encounter a power animal, or two or three, that want(s) to be united with you, to protect and care for you.
4. If you are suffering from pain or disease, she may be able to return body parts from your younger days when they were still healthy.

What you will perceive during the soul retrieval: first of all, Char smudges her instruments and all the people present with sage. She gives you a crystal or a shell to hold. She calls in the seven directions. Then she asks you some questions about your intent in doing this work, and about your past: what kind of accidents or traumas have occurred where you feel a part of yourself may have left, where do you perceive you need healing, where do you experience yourself as less than whole? Then she takes the crystal or the shell you have been holding; that is what she uses to collect the parts of your soul until she can return them to you. She lies down next to you on the floor, touching you at the shoulder, the hip and the ankle. The drumming starts, and as Char and her power animals go on their journey you will hear the sounds of her animals: the growl of the leopard, and the caw of the raven. As she does extraction work, Char will get up and rattle over you, sometimes touching you with her hands as she pulls out things that have been embedded into you, sometimes using her crystal to cut them away. She doesn't cut your skin as she does this, although some people do feel pain. You may find yourself experiencing a variety of feelings, and it is fine to laugh or cry, or move as you need to, but Char asks that you stay in the present: keep your eyes open and stay in touch with your allies (the other people you have chosen to be in the room). Do not journey with her.

Char usually has a pen and a piece of paper nearby so that she can make notes as she goes.

Welcome Home: When she is done, the drumming stops, and Char blows your soul parts into you. She then goes off on her own to write her experiences down, or she may talk from the notes she has already made, and let you have a tape of what she says. She will explain to you who she met on her journey, what she saw, what entities or archetypes came to help (or, occasionally, to hinder). You may take any of the information she gives you literally or metaphorically.

Life After Soul Retrieval: During the months after your soul retrieval you need to take care of your newly found parts of self. Celebrate them, listen to them, have fun with them and enjoy their perspective on your life.

Remember that they do not know who you are now; especially if they left a long time ago, they may be quite taken aback at the kind of life you are leading. You may experience some disorientation. Be patient with your selves. It is a good idea to build an altar with pictures of your children, and light a candle to them every day, welcoming them home. It may take a year or more to integrate your new parts.

When Heather and Terry arrived, I gave them the blurb to read, although Heather was an old friend of mine and I knew she was already aware of the information. Terry, under the gray mother cat's watchful eye, played with the three week old kittens that had been born inside the sofa. Char, friendly and warm as always, saged everything, and then, while the sage smoke lay thickly in my nostrils, she rattled, prayed, and called in the directions. She gave Heather a little crystal to hold while she interviewed her about past traumas she had been through that might have contributed to soul loss. Then she laid the soul retrieval blanket out on the floor. Heather lay down with Terry sitting to the left. Char took the crystal, and lay down on the right, with her arm over her eyes. I was standing holding Heather's drum, a heavy deep Irish one, with a beautiful tone. Now I began drumming as fast as the drumstick would go.

Almost immediately Char began to caw like a raven and make slight movements with her legs and arms. In a little while she sat up and rattled over Heather's belly, then felt for the crystal that lay on the floor to her right. Finding it, she knelt over Heather and sliced her aura open, *feeling* into her belly with her fingers, making vivid sounds like those of a bird or a cat. She pulled out some invisible thing which she then flung out towards the darkened window, and lay down again, using her right hand to feel Heather's shoulder. Over the drumming that filled the room, I heard her make more sounds. She sat up again and repeated her previous actions, except that this time whatever it was that she pulled out appeared to cover the whole upper torso, and was apparently heavy and large. That done, she felt for her notebook. I marveled that she could even relate to the concept of writing, for I could already tell she was far gone, her eyes half closed and glazed over, her red hair falling over her face. She brushed it back enough to scribble a quick note, and then lay down again. Soon she sat up to extract more unseen schmutz. The sweat was pouring visibly down her face, and she tore off her sweater, tossing it aside before she lay back down.

The drum was beginning to weigh heavily on me, and I felt panic flood over me that I would not be able to continue, though I knew from previous experience that I would. Terry, kneeling to Heather's left, held her free hand and smiled down at her, keeping her in the present. I watched as Char extracted more stuff, or paused to ask Heather a quick question, or made more notes. Sometimes I closed my eyes, letting myself fly on the sound of the drum, forgetting that it was I who pounded it. Time seemed to go on and on. Just when I was thinking that this really was a long soul retrieval and I must have been drumming for at least forty minutes, Char glanced at me and made a gesture of slicing her throat with her hand, which was my signal to stop. With a sigh, I knelt on the floor, letting go of the drum. Char got up and blew through the crystal into Heather's chest, then in the top of her head. That done, she sat on the sofa, saying, "Let me just have a cigarette and check my notes before I tell you what went on."

Heather moved to an unoccupied chair. I went into the kitchen and got everyone glasses of water. We all relaxed into the peaceful silence, with a sense of relief that Char seemed to have journeyed and returned unharmed, in spite of ordeals.

When she was ready, Char stubbed out her cigarette and moved into the middle of the little circle.

"For some reason, they want me to say what your power animals are first. The Turtle came, and she said, 'I am the Mother Earth, I am the divine Mother, and if you want to learn how to mother yourself, nurture yourself, and care for yourself, I am here to teach you that. I am also here to teach you how to have boundaries. There will be times when you need to kinda pull in, and work with how you think and feel about things, to gain authenticity. And there are times when you are gonna need to stick your neck out, and it is safe to do that. I am here to teach you that it is safe to mother yourself, which is pretty rocky stuff for you.'

"I have never returned a Turtle for anyone in my whole life. I giggled actually, she is so beautiful! She also said, take your time and you won't be disappointed, which I thought was kinda interesting.

"And the Bear came with the gifts of strength and purpose. She said purpose is very important to be looking at right now.

"We did a lot of extraction work, so lemme tell you about that. There was a lot of shame living in your body: a negative masculine presence on you from the incest you experienced, and some weird stuff connected to your vagina and your womb. Kind of going up and around your back. So we peeled him off of you. There were hands around your shoulders, so we took them away. Then, your mom was living in your throat, she was kind of just gestating and doing her thing, so we gave her another residence—we said, 'Here is another residence!'"

This was said with emphasis, and followed by Char's peals of raucous laughter, making the still air in the room shimmer. With a grin, Terry said, "Nice condo!"

"All this ancestral grief and anger in your lungs, it was really red in there. I did run into a lot of tarry stuff, that black gook you were talking about, we saw a lot of that. So my power animals pulled that out. And…terror. I saw that your mom had kinda handed you her terror in the form of a little kid. She was like this little kid living inside of you that wasn't you, this terrified seven year old."

She glanced down at her notes. "Oh yeah, this was weird: there was a bust of your mom's face over your shoulders and head, it reminded me of one of those busts you see, you know, like a bust of Caesar. It was just her bust, there was no heart, no power, no root, just the head stuff. So we pulled that off of you so you don't get stuck in any ancestral head trips."

Again her laughter rang round the room, but then she got serious immediately. "I thought that was very interesting! There was no heart, no solar plexus, which is power, no root, which is where thriving lives. Then there were blocks around your creativity given to you by your mom so you wouldn't be like your father. So we took those off of you. I though that was a trip, how *dare* she do that?"

Char sounded positively outraged. Heather shrugged.

"Then we took some kind of weakness out of your legs, I don't know what that was about. I don't know if you have arthritis. There was some kind of pain in your joints. So we pulled that out, I just saw it, so my animals went for it. Then there was sadness and some depression that was here—" she touched her heart area "—and coming out from your heart. There was a big heavy black box, that went from the top of your shoulder all the way down to your belly. It was just this very black box, not like a trunk, not like a real box where you could open it up and get in. It was solid. It was really bizarre and very heavy, so we pulled that out. It was blocking around your heart, like lead. Heavy hearted, I suppose that would be the best way to put it, someone else's heavy heartedness. *In* you, preventing you from experiencing lightheartedness.

"Then there was…" she paused, frowning down at the piece of paper "…stoi…stoc… *stoicism!*" She pronounced the word triumphantly, happy to have resurrected it successfully from her writing. "It was a mask that was given to you—you were told you can bear it, it'll be fine, just bear it, you'll be cool—but hey, now you know maybe you don't *have* to bear it! And it's cool that you are not cool! That felt like it came with a lover energy. I don't know when it showed up for you, I'm sure it started with your mother and then was transferred over to the lover that showed up.

"Then—" her voice dropped to whisper, and we could just hear her say, "Oh, my god, this was such a trip," before she spoke at normal volume again. "This was just my filter, I don't like to do a whole shitload of past life stuff, because we are dealing with this life, you know what I am saying? But you had one hand that was red. It was like a Native American lifetime, a life where you were Native American, and you died. It was a metaphor for you, I don't know what that means, I don't know what tribe it was, but you died, and you had a red hand from that life. So I took this red paint off your hand because you died in a way that wasn't good; it was a blessing to your tribe, but it wasn't good for you. It helped your tribe but it was a very hard death for you. So there was a belief that living and dying is a struggle, and we took that away. I might not have said it completely accurately, it is said through my filter, and that is the first time I have ever seen that. The red paint on your hand was preventing you from receiving all that you could. I thought that was bizarre. It'll be interesting to see what you are able to receive now." The bright eyed golden cat jumped up in her lap, and she stroked her. "Hi Fuzzy, I *love* you." The gray cat, her kittens momentarily abandoned, followed suit, seeing that Fuzzy was getting attention. "Sage is a good momma, yes, you are a great ally." She too received her share of strokes before Char returned her attention to the papers in her hand.

"OK, now for the soul parts you got back. The first thing we did was go to find the infant. Raven found your mom with the baby, who was you. Your mom was digging having a girl child, you know! But there was still a longing, even after she had you, there was still something missing for her, and she was thinking that you were going to heal her. So, when you were an infant, she took the soul part that enabled you to be emotionally and physically healthy. That's where all the slime has come from, that is where you got slimed. I saw you pretty brand new, maybe three months.

"So she wanted healing, and we wanted the baby. Give us the baby, hand the baby over, we said! Then my power animals gave her a healing. Mother Mary showed up on one side and Christ showed up on the other, and they said, 'We have the gift of compassion for you.' She was very excited about seeing them, she really wants their approval, even though she doesn't necessarily subscribe to it now. They said, 'We approve of you, get over it!'" We all joined her in laughing at this peculiar picture. "So they gave her the gift of compassion. And this most beautiful guardian angel came for you. She has been there for you since you were very little, and she didn't even want to show herself to me because she is just there for you. I don't subscribe to a lot of guardian angel stuff either, but it is really real for you. It's not something that shows up in a lot of soul retrievals. She said her name was Ariel, and she is about freedom and flying. She wants to fly, wants to party. Lots of angelic stuff showed up for you! The return of the infant returns to you the knowledge that you have the right to exist, and a sense of belonging, and also your personal emotional and physical health. Now you will be able to tell what is fulfilling for you in regards to personal emotional and physical health. Venus was holding the baby, she is so beautiful, and she was holding all the infinite potential of this child, all this infinite beauty. Aphrodite is another name for Venus, she is the goddess of love and beauty, and she gets what she wants. She can be a little bitchy too! She is boundary love. At least, that's my wild perceptions!

"Then—oh, this was so—" as Char got excited, her words began to jumble "—I was like, don't make me go there—there was just all of this stuff. It was the first time I had seen this, too. There were all these feathers falling, they were angel feathers, they were making you a bed out of their feathers! I was almost in tears about it. They were making this little bed for you. Then they said to me, now you have to go into this really dark place and at first I was like, oh no, don't make me go there! But I knew my Raven could do it, no problem. So it flew into this place where it was very dark and very cold, and there were all of these little kids in there, all very cold, shivering and shaking. I called your name, because I had to find you, and they all said, 'I'm Heather! I'm Heather!' And I said, 'No, no, no, no, I know you guys want to come home, but you aren't all Heather's soul parts!' I was looking for your eyes and for the shape of your face and your eyebrows, trying to work out what you would look like as a child, looking for identifying marks. Finally there was one little girl left, who was four years old, and she said, 'I'm her.' I said, 'Well, do you wanna come back?' And she said, 'Oh no, I would much rather be cold!' So I was like, 'OK, but I think that Heather can take you back now, I think she can take care of you and I don't think you will be cold any more, you will have warmth.' And so she said, 'OK! I'll go back.' She was a very very smart kid. She was checking it out to make sure it would be cool; really smart...and very pretty, I thought.

"Then I dropped some raven feathers for all the children, I knew I couldn't do a healing for all of them so I just dropped some feathers so they could do a little magic. Then Demeter came, and you were in this little nest of these white angel feathers. Demeter picked you up in this nest and was caring for you and holding you, she is the Earth Goddess. So Demeter is an ally for you too. The angelic presence was just huge, and I was also feeling some self-love from you at that point.

"Remember to ask questions if you have any." She looked at Heather questioningly, and Heather nodded.

"I can't say as I have ever really felt the presence of angels but…I am getting a growing sense that things are gonna be OK, over years."

"I know…these angels are so different, they just were really showing up for you. I have never seen them like that, it was pretty strange. I have certainly never seen them make a *nest* out of their wing feathers. I didn't even think they lost their wing feathers, I thought it was cosmically impossible!"

Heather echoed Char's laughter, saying, "Better not tell God! Give them some superglue!"

Char ran with her humor. "Yes, isn't there some universal law that they can't do that?"

"Maybe they need some angel Prozac or something!"

By this time we were all laughing, and Char told us, "The angels think that's funny too! Oh, then nested inside of you there was this little dead girl, just her bones. She had just her bones. That's why I sat up and asked if you have a deceased sister or someone that you are holding onto, because she was just all inside of you and it wasn't like she was alive, it was just her little bones. She didn't have any agenda or anything. I don't know why she was there. So we extracted her out, and then she was standing there and she was very upset, and *very* sad, so we gave her a little soul retrieval. We also gave her a present: we gave her a horse, which took her to the Land of the Dead, and then she was happy. Then Jenny, your ex-lover, asked for a life wish, because she wants to be more alive, so we did a healing for her, a little soul retrieval."

Heather interjected, confused, "So…what was it about Jenny? Was she the skeleton?"

"No! But when I did the mini soul retrieval for Jenny, I got the hit that the dead girl was connected with Jenny in some way, it was some girl who had died in her life. The girl is still really close to Jenny, and is very upset about being dead, she is like, 'Excuse the fuck out of me, I was busy!'" Char giggled at her characterization of the dead girl. "I don't know what the connection or disconnection is, but that's just what I saw, so I am going to honor it. It was preventing your ability to feel closeness, deep closeness and intimacy with the feminine. What Jenny returns to you—well, I mean what this *situation* returns to you, I don't know how to describe it, it is just the most bizarre thing—but what is returned to you from this situation is the ability to feel closeness again. Also, the ability to believe that you can make things better in a relationship, because I saw you reaching out to Jenny and trying to make things better, but you just couldn't seem to really reach deep enough, or really get to the core. There was a pain you couldn't reach, or a thing you couldn't make better, so letting go of that returns to you the knowledge that you can make things better. And also, a dragonfly showed up in this part, and there was also an angelic presence for the dead girl, and they gave the girl's skeleton a nest of feathers too. And it was interesting, because as soon as we removed the dead girl from you, she started to flesh out again. Her bones started to cover with flesh and with skin and with ligaments.

"And then there was also something living on the back of your horse. You said to me, 'There is something on the back of my horse that I need,' and there was this little star. That star was your empowerment. The horse said, 'She needs to have this all the time, instead of only having it when she is with me.' That was very cool! So I pulled the little star to your crystal, and that is returned to you.

"This was a really neat soul retrieval in a lot of ways, there was a lot of really neat unfamiliar symbolism for me." Glancing up from her notes, Char saw that I was eating almonds. "Hey, could I have a couple of those?" I passed her the bag and she stuffed a handful into her mouth, munching them audibly.

"So I was thinking it's about time for this soul retrieval to be over, especially because I got a little emotionally attached a couple of times, which is not normal for me, but what with the little children, and then the dead girl…I am so glad she was able to go to the Land of the Dead with the horse, and she was happy about that. After she left, we went to your mom and we were asking for your openheartedness—well, we didn't ask for it, she just had it, and I wanted to get any soul parts that would be beneficial for you—then all these people showed up for healings, and I kind of rolled my eyes a little bit. You know, I was like 'ohhhhh noooo!' but fortunately my Raven said, 'No problem, I'll do it.' So then these big fat fuzzy cute caterpillars came—and I guess I'm gonna tell you this—the people ate the caterpillars!"

"The people who wanted the healings?"

"Yes, they ate the caterpillars! And then they all turned into great big huge butterflies, the people did! It was so cool!" Char scrinched her face and giggled excitedly, delighted with the scenario. The rest of us, unfazed at the thought of them eating the caterpillars, joined her in hilarity. But Heather still had questions.

"Who were all these people?"

"They were your ancestors, and two ex-lovers, the two most recent. And the butterflies for your ancestors were about the ability to transmute old energies into compost, turn stuff into compost and grow things from it. Your mother started to like me OK too, she was like, 'Hmm, she is giving me something here, hmm, that's the lady with the Santa Claus bag.' I was like, 'Right on, babe!' That's how I want to be seen. Then your mom gave me your openheartedness, but there was something not quite right about it, something was attached, something was wrong. So Kali came, with all these weapons in all of her hands, because she is the goddess of destruction and creation. This is Kali." Char pointed to a picture on a nearby shelf, of an Indian goddess with many arms. "There was a dark shell around the openheartedness. Kali skillfully cut off the shell without harming the openheartedness inside, which was very cool. We gathered the openheartedness and returned it to you, so that you can be openhearted instead of close-hearted. That stuff was very old, I don't even know where it came from, but it was definitely *your* heart, and it was very tricky, it was a lot of trouble. Sorry!" She looked at Heather apologetically and shrugged.

Heather shrugged too. "Sounds like I should be the one apologizing!'

"Well, it's not your fault your mother is so wounded! But I haven't even finished yet, Kali had to come *again*, because your mom was doing some shit *again!* It was connected to safety, your mom gave me your heart, but it was still tainted in some way, there was still trickery in it. So Kali put the heart in her mouth—there were lots of people putting things in their mouths in this soul retrieval, everybody was eating everything—so Kali sucked all the icky stuff off of the heart, then she stuck out her tongue, and I could see just one little light. It was golden, and it was moving, and it was in the shape of a heart. That was about giving back to you your knowledge that it is *safe* to have a heart of gold. I have never returned that to anyone before, so that was very interesting. Kali is definitely an ally for you, she is like, 'I am your mother, I have all of this wonderful weaponry to protect you with, but I will never use it against you, I will always lay down my weapons with you, and be soft with you, I am the best mother.' That's what she said."

Char took a deep breath, and reached out to click the tape off. "So that is what happened in your soul retrieval, and this tape is for you."

"Well, I am probably going to have to listen to this tape again and again before I get it all!" Heather was obviously amazed at the amount and depth of information.

"Well, that's fine, you have a lifetime to do it in, that's what soul retrievals are about. They take a lifetime to integrate. That's what I like about them, they heal a lifetime. What's your therapist's name, Geri? It would be great if Geri could listen to it."

"Yeah, I am definitely going to take it to Geri and listen to it with her. Several things you have said have been like click click click…the dead girl must have been Tonya, Jenny's daughter. She died in a car accident just before Jenny and I became lovers."

"She was attached to your strength. She saw you as more powerful and she wanted power in the spirit world. She felt powerless there for some reason. The horse gave her the power to go to the next place in the spirit world."

"I find myself wondering if these people, like Jenny and my mother, will feel the effects of this."

"A lot of times people do. You never know what will happen…one person said her mom just called and yelled at her for three hours the day after her soul retrieval, because she knew something had changed. Sometimes people just know something is different. Once a woman showed up on my doorstep with her father, he had never done anything for her and now he bought her a car, he was suddenly being really nice to her. I didn't see a lot of stuff for you around your dad."

"You didn't?"

"Nuh huh…it was much more based on the feminine stuff."

"This stuff on receptivity, that was interesting. It's always been a hard thing for me to receive from people," Heather mused.

"That past life, oh, what a trip, that red right hand!" Char opened her eyes wide at the memory, speaking with reverence.

"I had no idea it was all going to be so interesting!"

"Yeeeeah! It's fun, huh? I think there might be more fear of it being exciting than it *not* being exciting. But it's great to be exciting!" She laughed joyfully as she turned towards Heather's ally. "Terry, do you wanna share anything as an ally?"

"Well, I was just glad to be here. I haven't seen Heather for a long time and I'm hoping you will be around a little more now." She grinned broadly at Heather and reached out to touch her hand. "It's interesting, because we were just looking at old pictures of you, when you were four."

"I did see you leave at age four, but I didn't see why you left. You were just out of here: 'OK, I gotta go now!' Terry, you rock, thank you very much, you are a superstar! What about you, Mikaya? Boy, that drum was fantastic, it just took me!"

"Yeah, it was amazing! Very heavy, I thought my arm was going to fall off. Next time I'll have it propped up somehow. Char, I wanted to ask you, didn't I see you blow some things into her as you were doing the soul retrieval as well as afterwards?"

Chat paused for a moment, thinking. "Yes, you did, that was her new lungs. They are beautiful new pink lungs. But they are very small, so they gotta grow, they gotta be given some time to grow. We extracted a lot of black tarry stuff, and there was a need for newness, something new to take its place."

Heather nodded as though she understood this. "Well, it was great to have you two, Mikaya and Terry, as allies, because I don't think it would have worked to have had people I didn't know so well. I needed people who had seen me go through a lot of my changes."

Char nodded. "Your body is gonna be different. It changes on a deep level, on a molecular level, a DNA level. You wanna make sure to—" she paused to cough and said, "Eugh, my voice is starting to go—you wanna make sure to take really good care of yourself right now. That color lavender you are wearing, that might be a really good color for you. You might want to smell lavender a lot too, it will make you feel restful. And wear things that are tangerine colored, that will help you to remember lightheartedness. Don't use tangerine in your office ever, no work gets done where you have tangerine colors! Your soul parts may need nurturing, that baby may need to be held a lot, so put your arms around yourself and hold yourself. There may be times when you just want to lay down and do that. A common report with infant soul parts is that people just space out. Your infant just doesn't know about practical stuff and finds everything really big and amazing. It's like, 'Wow, what happened while I was away?' So remember to mother her, and look both ways before you cross the road! You also have a lot of soul parts back from the time you spent with Jenny, so there are parts of you wrapped up with her that you won't recognize without her. You may find yourself saying things you really didn't intend to say."

She nodded, coughing again, and we all stood up to go, seeing that she needed to rest.

Chapter Eleven

It was 9.45, time to call the class to an end.

"OK, so that's it for today! I'll see you all next week." Char smiled radiantly round at her four students as they started to pull their things together, then she got up and walked into the kitchen to put the kettle on. She came out again to say goodnight. As she put her arms around Elisabeth to give her a hug, Char realized that she was needed in some way and pulled back with a question in her eyes. Elisabeth looked slightly embarrassed. "Char, I was talking with my sisters and my mother the other day and we think maybe we have a curse on the female side of the family."

Immediately Char knew she was right, not even knowing if it was something she just realized or something she had always been aware of. "Mmmmm!" she nodded, raising her eyebrows in agreement.

"Well, we were wondering if you could do anything about it…"

"I'm sure I can! Why don't you call me and set up a time for you all to come here? I would want all four of you, your sisters and your mother."

It was only a day or two later when Diana, Elisabeth's mother, called, and because they were friends, Char agreed to see them soon, rather than make them go on her three month waiting list. So they arranged to be at Char's house the day before Thanksgiving, which was normally a day that Char would take off. That morning I had brunch with her, a friend (Christine), and her mother (Matilda). Char had made peace with her mother many years earlier, and they often did shamanic work together. As we sat at the table in the restaurant waiting for our food, Christine, who was always interested in Char's work, asked, "What are you going to do to lift this curse?"

"It'll be extraction work," replied Char, taking a generous sip of her mocha latte. "It'll look like a soul retrieval, I guess. I don't know what these things normally look like!" She shrugged and laughed, then turned to Christine, saying more seriously, "I was hoping you would drum for me?"

"Oh!" Christine was clearly surprised. "Well...I'd love to...but I don't have any experience."

"Yes, you do, you drummed for Linda's soul retrieval the other day!" Char contradicted her.

"Well, that wasn't much! I was thinking you would ask Matilda or Mikaya—"she nodded across the table "—they have much more experience than me!"

I shook my head, a little sadly, since I enjoy working with Char. "Sorry, I have other arrangements."

Char looked at her mom. "Why don't you and Christine both drum for me? Christine can borrow my drum, do you have yours? There are four of *them*, it seems like there ought to be more than one drummer on my side! As a matter of fact, I was thinking of having a fourth person there to help, I want to ask Tim as well." She reached for the bread and absently passed Christine a piece as she took her own.

Matilda nodded, pleased to be asked, though acting cool. "I could do that. How long do you think it will take?"

"Well, the drumming will probably only take maybe thirty minutes or so. I won't have to spend that long talking with them beforehand since they've all had soul retrievals already, except for Maria, the youngest sister. The others will've filled her in." She looked up at the ceiling, thinking. "So maybe two hours total."

"That means three!" interjected Christine, laughing, and Char smiled down at her plate with a look of slightly woeful resignation.

Matilda grinned knowingly. "Yes, I know about Char's sense of time!"

"You *should* do, I got it from you!" was Char's quick response.

Matilda looked both amused and doubtful. "Well, I'm not so sure about that, but anyway I can certainly be there."

"Is there anything I should know about dual drumming? I mean, I've never done this before. Are you sure you wouldn't be better off without me?" Christine was nervous about executing her responsibilities adequately.

"Oh, I'm sure you can do it!" Matilda waved her hand dismissively. "All you have to do is watch me. And I think that for something like this it'll be really good for Char to have more than one drummer. The drum beat is what keeps her on course, so it's always good if it's strong and clear and loud and steady. I imagine Char will want us either side of the action so that she feels surrounded by the sound. So just keep an eye on my drum and match your beat to mine. And it won't matter if you get out of sync, so don't get anal about it."

Char nodded. "Yes, I've had all sorts drumming for me, people with gammy hands that drop the drum half way through, tapes that run out in the middle, little people…whenever someone has a kid there, they always want to do the drumming and I always let them cuz I just have such a soft spot for kids—" she laughed "—but they can never really keep it up fast and steady enough for long. It should be really fast if it is going to carry me, as fast as you can make it, so it'll just be great to have drumming that I know will last."

"Well, OK, then…what time are we starting?"

"I think I said six—oh, damn!" Char frowned and sucked in her lip. "I just realized Tim will be working tonight." She shrugged and brightened up, dismissing the problem. "Oh well, it'll all work out exactly as it's meant to!"

Just then Christine's cell phone rang. She dived for her jacket pocket and pulled it out, turning away from the other two so as not to interfere with their conversation. But Char was smiling; she already knew it was for her.

"Hallo, Tim! We were just talking about you!" Christine turned back towards Char with a rueful grin. "Well, I can't believe you asked me if I am working with Char tonight—she just said she wants me to drum for her! If you're saying I should be there too, I guess I had better pay attention, you are the third person who has said so in five minutes! Here, here's Char for you!" She handed the phone to Char, and said to Matilda, "I don't know why I ever question what Char says. She always knows what she's doing!"

Meanwhile Char was chatting to Tim. When she was done she said goodbye, and handed the instrument back to Christine, who glanced at the battery gauge, muttering, "Funny how it's always more charged after you've been using it."

Char laughed. "Well, I guess Tim is getting very good at receiving my messages! He says he will be available for help from his office tonight if I need it, he will just withdraw from his work for a few minutes. Dan is working with him on a client, so they ought to be able to manage OK if he has to take a break. So that's cool! I must say it's a relief to know all my allies are coming through!" She grinned broadly at the two of them and took another mouthful of chicken salad. "Anyway, Mom, he says—and I think he is undoubtedly right—that I need to make sure that I have a way out, since there are four of them. So I think I need to position myself so they are on each side of me, and then if I need to get out I can go straight up. What do you think?"

Matilda nodded thoughtfully. "Sounds good to me…you can have two of them either side of you with their heads in the middle."

Brunch over, I wished them all luck, and said goodbye. They had other things to do, and didn't arrive back at Char's house until Diana, Kay, Maria and Elisabeth were drawing up in their car. Char laughed with her usual spontaneous joy.

"Look at you all! Four wonderful women and they are all coming to my house! Oh, I am so blessed!" She gave each of them a hug before she introduced Matilda and Christine, who sedately shook hands. They went indoors, and arranged themselves around the living room. For half an hour or so they talked about the curse and how they had all seen it manifesting: how every one of the last three generations of mothers had had one girl child, and how each mother had systematically abandoned the girl child, and then gone crazier and crazier in their old age.

"Now I know I haven't followed those patterns," said Diana, "But I still feel like we all exhibit some of them, like we all have terrible trouble maintaining relationships with men—" the three younger women around her nodded vehemently "—and we choose such awful men to get into relationships with!"

"Yes," said Elisabeth, "I mean, I have done a lot of work on myself and I know that these guys are not worth my time but I still feel irresistibly attracted to them! I just keep wondering, what is going on, why does this keep happening? Our ancestors were pretty loony, and we are all afraid of going crazy. I think if I had got married at a young age and had kids, I would have gone crazy like them. They all drank too, I have already given up my addictions, and made some changes, but I still feel like some other force is at work here."

"And it's not even just relationships," chipped in Maria, the youngest, "I feel so blocked in everything I do, it seems much harder for me to get things done than it does for other people. I always have far more problems to deal with, and they come up out of nowhere!"

Char nodded slowly, and made a few notes on her pad. "OK...well, I'll see what I can do. Do you know anything about your past, do you know of anyone who might have put a curse on your family?"

Diana shook her head, but she reached in her pocket. "I don't know much about the details of our past beyond what I have already told you, but I remembered this." She produced a photo which she laid on the table. "Look, this is my great grandmother and my grandmother and my mother, don't they all look crazy? This is when they were living in New England. I was the first to come out west."

Char studied the photo, taking it over to the light to look at it more carefully. Then she put it down decisively, saying, "OK, well, now I am going to pray, and then I need all four of you to lie on the floor head to head and I will lie in the middle. Here, let me get soul retrieval blankets for you to lie on."

She disappeared and returned in a moment with four heavy patterned blankets, all with different pictures. Two had large wildcats on them in different poses, one had a flock of birds, and the last had a single eagle soaring over mountains. She lit the sage in a shell, fanning it with the huge blue heron feather that she had just been given. The herb burned brightly, so that soon all the tools and all seven people were thoroughly soaked in smoky clouds. Only occasional jokes and spurts of laughter broke the respectful silence. Sitting on the sofa, Char closed her eyes and turned to each direction asking for guidance, and calling in the energies and archetypes. That done, she laid the blankets out on the floor, so the four women could lie down as she had suggested. Meanwhile she organized Matilda and Christine so they were on either side of the group on the floor. When she was satisfied, she lay down in between the four women, signaling the drumming to begin.

Immediately dual beats filled the apartment and she was no longer lying there, but instead found herself in a canoe with two of the women ahead of her and two behind. Each of them had a clear cord coming from them to something or someone unseen. Snow Leopard stood looking forward in the bow of the boat and Raven flew alongside, cawing encouragingly. For a little while things seemed quite calm as they made their way between banks that were distant and misty. Abruptly, they were somewhere else, somewhere unnameable. Within the eyes of Snow Leopard, she encountered an ancestor, one of the women from the photo, clearly deceased, who seemed to be controlling all the cords. She tried to talk to her, but the atmosphere was uncomfortably hot, and she felt distracted. Just as she was wondering what to do about that, she realized her sense of the drumming was fading in and out. *That's not right,* she thought, *I should be able to hear the drumming clearly just like I did before.* Then she found herself looking up, and quite a different picture came into view. In the center, above her head, was a strange round thing, dark and thick. Out of it came a network of cords to each of the daughters, but the main cord, the one that held the round thing in its central position, appeared to come from the mother. She looked closer, and followed one of the cords from the mother; it went back to the ancestor from the photo, who was watching what was going on. Char tried to reach out again, but realized she was still in the middle of the four women and could not move. She tried to lift herself up out of the network of cords, only to discover they had trapped her within them, and she could not grip any of the cords to break them—every time she tried, the cord she was reaching for just seemed to dissolve in her grasp, and would reappear elsewhere. She looked around and saw that each of the four women was covered with a shadowy cocoon that boxed them in. She was helpless to reach them. Again she was aware of being too hot, and she could barely hear the drumming at all now. She began to feel frustrated, more and more so as she tried again and again to escape. Where were her power animals? They didn't seem to be nearby, as they should be, and as they normally were.

She had not reckoned how strong the ancestral ties would be with a mother and three daughters. Feeling panic rise, she made herself calm down, thinking, *it's OK, this is a good day to die, what better way to die than this?* But she wanted out. *What on earth had made her think she could do this on her own?* Then she remembered she didn't have to do it on her own, and she was aware of calling for Tim in her head.

> *Dan and Tim were working on a client who lay comatose on the table between them. It was the third time that they had done this kind of work together—an experiment in combining their skills to remove energy blocks. Quite suddenly, Tim felt an unseen tug, and realized Char was calling him. He dropped his hands off the woman's belly and took a step or two backwards. Dan glanced up fleetingly and then, immediately perceiving that Tim didn't need him, he returned his attention to the client. Quietly and calmly as a cat, Tim walked over and stood by his altar, eyes open, yet unseeing. He felt drained but not in an unpleasant way, just a sense of his strength—his allies—being elsewhere. No thought passed through his brain as silent words of prayer flowed out of him into unseen places. Then, as his strength flowed back into him, he felt it was complete, and he turned back to the woman he had been working on. He had no idea what had been happening. He didn't need to know right then—he would hear about it later.*

Immediately, Char was flooded with Tim's strength, and she felt her own cords sinking firmly into the earth that she knew so well. With great relief, she sensed the presence of Raven and Snow Leopard. The sound of the drumming surged up around her again, and a pleasantly cool breeze dried the sweat on her skin. She knew she was safe, although the black cords still surrounded her. Without any thought, she leaned forward close to the cord nearest to her, and blew on it. At once it became solid, and this time, when she put her hand out, it didn't melt away. Breaking it in half, she continued blowing on and breaking each of the cords that held her. Soon she was free. She approached the ancestor through the eyes of Raven, hearing her own words, "We need to take this cord back now." The old lady tightened her grip and withdrew a little, muttering. Char heard someone say in a kindly tone, "Would you like a healing?" The ancestor relaxed as though soothed by the offer of help. Char saw an image of someone else, another lady, young and vibrant, though Char could tell she was long deceased, yelling at the great great grandmother in hatred and anger, then sprinkling herbs over a charcoal fire as she whispered spells. A handsome young man stood in the background, and Char looked away; she didn't need to know these details. Snow Leopard gave the grandmother a healing, and very soon the cord going back to Diana shriveled and disappeared. At the same time the cocoons that cloaked each of the four women began to melt until they were completely gone.

She herself then turned to Diana, saying, "You need to let all these cords to your children go. They are adults now, and they need to lead their own lives." The mother needed no further telling; in a moment the cords to the three younger women had shriveled, and they were no longer attached to Diana or to the old relative. The dark ball that had acted to pull together all the central strands was gone.

Within the mother there still lay three individual lights, and Char knew that each of those lights belonged to each of the daughters. Three little butterflies swam into her vision and each took one of the lights. The green one went back to Kay, the blue one to Elisabeth and the yellow one to Maria. Diana was left with a warm angelic presence.

Aware of her exhaustion now, Char felt great relief when the canoe grounded itself on the bank. As she felt the beloved ground under her, and saw the women on the floor around her, she signaled to the two drummers. Sound faded away into a real, peace-filled silence. Slowly she sat up and pulled herself onto her feet, brushing her hair back off her face. The four women around her began to stir. Slightly surprised how easily her legs carried her, she strolled out onto the deck and flopped into a chair. She put a cigarette in her mouth, and then Christine was kneeling beside her with a lighter.

"Oh sweetheart, thanks!" She took a long deep drag. "I'll go in and talk to everyone in a minute. First I have to cool down. How was the drumming?" She laughed at Christine's woeful face. "Did you feel like you lost it?"

"Yes, it was fine to begin with, and then there was this fog that came over me and I couldn't see Matilda's drum! At first we were so much in sync it was wonderful, and then the connection between us got all fuzzy and thick!"

"That's OK, sweetie, you did great. Everything got fuzzy and thick. Mom was losing it too. There was some very strong energy there, I lost it for a while."

"I was worrying about you. Then suddenly I thought of Tim, and as soon as I thought of him I could see again, and after that it was OK."

"Yes, I called him into the circle. I needed another practitioner. I am so glad he was available. Isn't he wonderful?" She laughed. "I remember the first time I saw him he was radiating golden light so brightly I could barely make out his features! He came for a reading when he was still working with computers, and I could see so clearly that he was doing healing work that I could hardly believe he wasn't. But he really wasn't, he had this high-powered job with computers. I'm so glad he is doing the work now, he is so talented. If he had refused to do it, all that talent would've atrophied. What a waste!"

Back in her living room, she told the four women about her experiences. After they had expressed their gratitude, paid her, and left, she fell onto her bed into a deep and well-earned sleep.

Chapter Twelve

When Storme and her partner Sally first moved to the Seattle area, they had a house-warming. One of their friends had her own idea about what they should do to warm their house.

"I met this great woman recently, you should get her to come and do a house blessing for you. She is really good!"

Storme's initial response was not enthusiastic. "I'm used to all these people who use crystals, read books and then think they can move spirits around—I mean, *I* know how to move energy! I know how to do that really well, I've studied that with my Wiccan teacher."

But her friend was insistent. "No, really, Storme, this woman is the real thing. You should meet her."

In the end Storme called to make an appointment. As soon as Char walked through the door, Storme knew from the energy around her that this woman was for real, and sure enough, she was able to tell them things that no one else knew. She pinpointed a spot in the house where the couple had had a really nasty argument. At that time, Storme was very secretive about her private life, and she hadn't told anyone about the argument.

When Char left, they gave her some home-made cedar incense and food in a basket. As she thanked them, she picked up the incense with interest and said, "Did you make this? Can I buy this to sell in my store?"

Storme laughed, shaking her head. "Not unless you can wait six months! I don't have any more and I can't get it until November on the full moon, when I go pick it in the forest, and then I don't actually make it until December, so I couldn't get it to you until January."

To Storme's surprise, she didn't get the usual response: why can't you just go out and pick it now? Char nodded as though she understood, saying, "OK!"

Over the next year they saw each other occasionally and slowly became friends. Char and Sally hit it off especially well. They began to help with soul retrievals—Sally would sit with the client, keeping her present, while Storme drummed. To begin with, Storme didn't realize the importance of focusing on the drumming, but in time she learned to be less scattered, and the soul retrievals went more quickly and efficiently as a result. She learned how to clean off the drums and other instruments after they had been used; she could feel as soon as she touched them if they had something yucky attached to them.

One evening they were in Denny's late at night. Char looked across the table at Storme, and said, "Spirit has told me to say this, I am to offer you a private apprenticeship."

Storme wasn't one to jump into something without knowing what it meant, but by now she had spent enough time with Char to know this was an opportunity she wouldn't meet anywhere else. Still, she hesitated. "Well, I am not saying no, because that would be crazy, but I need to know more about what this means."

"Well, think about it, ask me any questions you have, and we'll go from there."

After they talked for a couple of hours, Storme said yes. That was the last time Char told her to feel free to ask—as an apprentice, Storme soon learned she was expected to accept what Char said without question. It wasn't a method of learning that Storme took to easily, and sometimes she felt that she was a very slow learner, trying her teacher's patience. But spirit had told Char to teach her, and as Char told Storme many times, she never said no to spirit.

The very first morning Storme turned up at Char's house to begin the apprenticeship, Char said, "OK, we are going outside to pray."

At that time, Storme didn't realize that praying was a basic way of life for Char. She was shocked, and a little defiant. She had grown up going to church, praying to a Christian God, and she wasn't going to start doing that again now. She said, "I don't pray!"

Char looked at her with a hint of amusement and no trace of impatience. "Well, you're going to begin now."

Outside in the garden, Char had her gather stones which they used to make a medicine wheel. Then she told her about the directions, and they started in the middle of the circle, facing east with their hands out, while Char prayed. Storme turned when Char did, and looked up when she did, and touched the ground when she did, but her head was reeling with all this information. How would she ever get all this? She had read Sun Bear's books and Kenneth Meadow's books, but they were from a different tribal tradition. Later, Char told her to make a medicine wheel in her yard, and she began to understand that learning how to pray in the medicine wheel was a deeply personal thing, the basis of all other work. Within a year, it was a daily ceremony for her to ask for help from the directions and thank each of them in turn. She did it outside whenever she could, since she found that being able to feel the wind, see the sky and touch the ground made it all more present for her.

Char taught her a song that she was to sing four times in each direction, starting in the east, after saying the prayer. It was a while before Storme came out of herself enough to sing freely and clearly, without worrying what the neighbors were thinking. In the long run, though, she found that singing and praying together were very powerful. She understood that it was putting out energy and intent more strongly, so therefore she got a lot more back. The song was a gift of gratitude to the ancestors, a healing for the Earth. She began to sing almost daily, and found it very soothing.

There were times in the first year when Storme was at Char's house every day for hours, learning not only how to be a medicine person but also how to do soul retrievals and house blessings, and how to do the pipe. Looking around her house, seeing the eagle feathers, coyote claws, bearskin, blue heron feathers, and many other natural tools that were used in the medicine work, Storme got a little anxious. One day she said to Char, "These tools are really important, they really help with the focus, but how am I going to get any for myself? I mean, I can't go out and buy this stuff, where am I supposed to get them from?"

Char often laughed, but then she laughed the loudest and longest that Storme had ever heard, only laughing harder when Storme, a little put out, asked her, "What are you laughing at? What's so funny?"

She told her student, "I saw you finding all these gifts in Nature, and I knew that it's something you don't have to worry about at all, because they will all come to you easily."

Of course Char was right: the tools Storme needed always turned up for her. When she found an animal carcass with parts that she could use, Char taught her to listen to the spirit of the animal, and do what it told her. Once she ordered her to sleep with the body of a hawk by her pillow, much to Sally's dismay.

Char was very strict about leaving an offering whenever something was taken. So Storme would leave tobacco, and say prayers for the animals. Gradually she learned to let go of her scarcity mentality, understanding that all things would come to her when she could trust in the infinite generosity of the universe. She began to realize how deeply we are all related: the star nations, the four leggeds, the insects, the two leggeds, all who walk on Mother Earth. There must be equal respect for all of us, and then all of us will have what we need. People are afraid they won't have enough love, but love and respect grow whenever they are honored. There is not a limited source of them.

Over time, Char taught Storme how to make power necklaces, medicine pouches, and rattles. Medicine tools look like art, but the intention is very different. Storme would sometimes be in constant focus all day long, praying and smudging to gain clarity, to make sure her intention was very clear as she worked on a piece. She couldn't lie around watching TV, as she would have done if she was just beading for the sake of art.

She learned to relate to her power animals on a daily basis, since she worked with them often. As she opened to spirit, she found it sometimes got very noisy, with many entities vying for her attention. Char taught her how to tell spirits to be quiet and go away, letting them know that she would give them time when she had time. They were not allowed to harass her.

When one of the year-long classes started, Storme joined, and got to watch (sometimes enviously, since she herself was not allowed to ask questions like others were) how Char taught different people, tuning into each individual's needs. Studying the Major Arcana of the Tarot taught her a great deal, and when they started doing practice readings on each other, Storme saw how the work she had done on the archetypes was not just for her own personal growth, but so that she would better understand human nature, and better be able to translate what she was seeing psychically into useful terms for the client.

Storme was a very private person. Before she met Char she didn't talk to people when she was having a hard time, she just pretended that everything was fine. One day Char said to her, "When I ask you how you are, I expect you to tell me."

Storme looked surprised. "I *have* told you, I'm fine!"

"No, you're not, you've been having arguments with Sally because she's interested in someone else."

Storme was speechless. For a few moments silence reigned, then she said, "Has Sally been talking to you?"

Char laughed. "No, I've been inside your head. You're my apprentice, it's my job to keep tabs on you."

That was the first time Storme realized this was possible. From then on she tried to be aware of times when Char was in her head, though she usually didn't know it. Occasionally Char would send her messages: she would just become aware that there was something she must do, such as pick up a particular item when she was on her way to Char's house. She found she had to be really clear to get these messages; if she was preoccupied with her own worries, then she missed them. Under Char's tutelage, she learned how to go inside other people's heads. She went into Char's a few times, finding it uncomfortably fast. She couldn't get used to Char's high zippy energy. When she was doing a reading or a soul retrieval, she sometimes went in other people's heads, and found them really varied: some happy, some painful, some warm, some friendly, some contained and controlled. The worst ones for her were those that had pain locked away in little rooms and boxes. That was not fun.

This kind of going into someone's head was similar to journeying. Like many people, she had journeyed naturally as a child, utilizing what we call the astral realm, flying to jungles and mountains. Like many adults, she had lost that ability as she grew up, but now she recovered it fairly fast. She practiced lying down in her room, and *traveling* to see what her girlfriend was doing in the back of the house. Then she would physically go there to see if she was right. It was the same kind of thing as journeying to the underworld, which she did during soul retrievals, but safer; she knew that she wasn't likely to meet weird and dangerous things when she was just journeying around her own house. As her abilities improved, she could split off a piece of her consciousness to go somewhere while she was busy in the physical arena, although that required a high level of concentration.

One evening, a few months into the apprenticeship, Storme went to bed feeling uncomfortable, although she was unable to pinpoint what the discomfort was about. Hearing her dog walk around the house, which was very unusual behavior for him at night, she got up, to discover the dog had peed in every room, in little circles. He would only do that if he was scared. She was puzzled: what was there to be frightened of? She checked everywhere and still couldn't see anything wrong. When she went back to bed, she began to experience a sensation of being strangled. The feeling grew stronger and stronger until it was seriously uncomfortable. Sally did everything she knew to help, to no effect. Finally, Storme managed to choke out instructions to call Char, although it was one in the morning by then.

Fortunately, Char picked up the phone, and her response to Sally's anxious request for help was immediate. "Who is it?"

Then Storme remembered to look in the other realms, where she saw a slender tall man with a bald patch and thinning gray hair, tied back in a pony tail. He was making fun of her: "I'm stronger than you!"

When Sally repeated Storme's strangled description, Char laughed without humor. "Well, I suppose you were due a visit from my dad, since he always checks out my apprentices!"

Once Keith had been identified, he left of his own accord and when Storme recovered, she deliberately addressed him, telling him he was not welcome in her house or anywhere near her or any of her friends or family. He didn't return. But it was a powerful lesson for Storme, since she had never believed that spirits could have physical effects.

Char taught Storme that it was very important to say the first thing that came into her mind when she was reading someone, even if it seemed totally off the wall. Those first hunches, that have not been tainted by our mental talk, are often remarkably correct. It's also very necessary to phrase things positively. People often gravitate towards what is negative, failing to ask about the good stuff. Char was adamant that whatever one saw, it was vital to express it to a client in a way that would promote the highest good, helping the client to appreciate the beauty of life. That meant the reader was always making judgment calls about how to say things, and what not to say, and what to emphasize.

Storme began to understand how important it was to let the client talk. That was part of their cleansing, and it was her job to be a good listener. She also learned how to see people with empathy and compassion, letting go of judgment. This was one of the hardest lessons, because in order to let go of judgments of others, she had to look at herself. In the end, her apprenticeship changed her on every level: spiritually, emotionally, mentally and physically. She was forced to address her own issues, that might otherwise blind her. She had to get out of the way, and become a hollow bone for spirit to walk through. She had to walk through her own fear in order to understand that whenever someone needs healing, there is always some aspect of fear at work. This was a revelation for Storme, since she had previously believed that some people were just jerks; she had never grasped that they might be motivated by fear of loss or pain.

Some of the most life-changing lessons Char gave her were simple questions, such as, *what is power?* Storme was to write her answer and give it to her teacher when she was done, but Char never told her how much she was to write, never asked how she was doing with it, and never gave her any hints on what angle to take. This was a traditional apprenticeship, and the tradition was that the student should experience the lesson and figure it out herself, by praying, by looking inside. Char was not looking at the *answers* that Storme gave her to see whether she'd got it or not, she was looking at her behavior.

Hubris was one of the most difficult; it was eight months before Char let go of that. Early on, Storme casually mentioned that she had looked up the dictionary definition of the word on line. Char laughed long and hard, and then said, "OK, there will be no more of that!" Eventually Storme understood that the most important thing about hubris is being able to *not* have it, which means being willing to take a back seat and listen to others without jumping to conclusions and making judgments.

The authenticity lesson was also a continuing thread, and Storme finally realized that it always would be, that she would always be examining herself to make sure she was coming from an authentic place. When Char first wrote down the question for her—*what is authenticity?*—she wrote in response, "something that is real, not fake." Char ripped up the paper and wrote again, *what is authenticity?* Apparently dissatisfied with all Storme's other attempts, she told her to talk into a tape recorder every day for thirty days, saying what authenticity is. That made Storme think about it constantly. After the fifteenth day, she was finding it hard to not to repeat herself. When she turned the tape in to her teacher, Char said nothing, as always, and it was another six months before Storme understood that she had to stop looking to her teacher for validation, but look within herself, knowing that she would have the answer when she found herself living it.

One day, she walked through the door of Char's house, drum in hand, ready for a scheduled soul retrieval. Char greeted her with the usual warm hug, saying, "Did you get me some sage?"

"No, I thought about it, but you didn't tell me I needed to get it."

Char laughed. "Yes, I did, sweetie, you just didn't hear me."

Storme metaphorically kicked herself for not trusting the voices inside her head. She raised her eyebrows apologetically. "Sorry!"

"OK, we'll go out and get some later, I think I have enough right now. Storme, I want you to start talking without using any pronouns!" Char smiled at her as she reached for the cigarettes on the mantelpiece.

Storme stared at her, frowning as she tried to compute what this meant. "You mean, don't use the word, *I*?"

"Don't use *I, we, she, you, her, he, it, mine, ours, her, them*—don't use any pronouns!" She tore the wrapping off the cigarette packet, throwing it into the empty fireplace behind her.

"You mean, just when I am with you?"

"No, all the time!"

"Hmmm...what do I say instead of pronouns?"

"You use your name or the other person's name."

When she got home, Storme tried this out on Sally. "Char's told me—no, she's told Storme!—that I have to talk without using any pronouns. No, I mean, Char's told Storme—no, Storme means that Char has told her not to use—damn! This is going to be hard. Let's start again. Char has told Storme that Storme is not to use pronouns!"

By this time Sally was in stitches of laughter, and indeed, Storme often found that her attempts to talk were seen as hilarious. People who didn't know her well just thought she was very peculiar. She did feel embarrassed, but she also found it exhausting to talk, since she had to think so hard about how to phrase what she wanted to say, that it seemed barely worth saying anything. She spent a lot of time listening, and discovered that most people talk about themselves. After two weeks, frustrated but somewhat wiser about human interactions, she gave up, and Char didn't insist she continue.

By now Storme journeyed easily, which was an infinite source of assistance to her. She could lie down somewhere quiet and dark, and connect with spirit whenever she needed help. One of her projects was to write a story of a medicine woman on birth, death and rebirth. This was a winter lesson, so she was praying often to the North, and connecting with the Grandmothers. What did it mean to be a medicine woman? It made her look at who she wanted to become and who it was Char wanted her to be. The Grandmothers talked to her about it, and she began to write. She wrote and rewrote, until finally she came up with a poem that satisfied her. She didn't want to use ordinary paper, so she got a piece of parchment paper that was round. It felt like it needed to be a circle since they were talking about the circle of life. Then she burned the end of a piece of cedar, so that she could write with it. When the laborious process was finally done, she gave it to Char, feeling quite pleased with herself. Of course, Char never said a word about it. But doing it, and learning from it, had been a gift, and she was beginning to let go of her desire for feedback, knowing that if Char thought she hadn't got the lesson, it would come up again.

One day when Storme was not home, her teacher came over and left a note in her workshop. She found it later that day: it read simply, "In the next three months, make an authentic Lakota buffalo rattle." She had no idea how to do this, and she knew she wasn't allowed to ask questions. Utilizing every possible source of research, she found out about all kinds of rattles, but not a buffalo rattle. After two months she was getting some visions, but they were not as clear as she needed, and, aware that she only had one more month, she was getting anxious. Finally, when she was over at Char's house one day, Char handed her a small box.

"This is to help you with the rattle. Only use it if you have to!"

Back at home, Storme carried the box into the house, placing it carefully in front of her altar. She busied herself with other things, but kept coming back to look at the box and touch it, wanting to open it, but stopping herself. Praying in front of the altar gave her no clarity. When Sally came home from work, she was still fretting. "What do you think, should I open it, should I leave it?" she asked anxiously.

Sally shrugged. "I dunno!" A couple of hours later, as Storme was still wandering around the house full of doubt, Sally turned to her impatiently, and said, "Just open it!"

Storme frowned and pursed her lips. "I don't know!" Before she went to bed that night, she gave in to her torment, knowing she would never sleep for thinking about it. Sitting crosslegged on the floor, she put the box in her lap and carefully opened it. Inside were some beads and coyote claws. She rubbed her forehead, tipping her baseball cap back, and muttered, "What am I supposed to do with these?"

Eventually she began, trusting her inner self. Taking a piece of wood, she carved it into a handle, then made the rattle head out of rawhide, putting beads and a crystal inside it. She indented the coyote claws into the handle so they didn't stick out. When she turned it in, Char lifted it, shook it and examined it as her apprentice stood by. "What did you put inside?" she asked.

"Fifty two beads and one crystal." Storme tried to hide her anxiety.

Char nodded. "OK! There is just one thing wrong—" she pointed out the claws on the handle "—these should be attached to the top of the rattle. They are the buffalo horns."

Relief surged through Storme's body. She had it pretty much right! She took the rattle home and removed the claws from the handle, gluing them onto the top of the rawhide.

Having a fulltime apprentice was a fulltime job for Char, since any such person was inevitably central to her existence. So she was very happy when, after three years, Storme was about to be released. She was relishing the prospect of getting her life back. Two weeks before the ritual for the end of Storme's apprenticeship, she sat with Christine at the dining room table, still cluttered with last night's dishes. They both found it easy to ignore them as they hugged their coffee mugs and chatted. Christine was in a good mood too, telling Char a story about yesterday's job interview. Char listened with ninety percent of her attention; the other ten percent was tuned into the spirits who occupied various spots in the room. There were none she wasn't familiar with, so nothing distracted her overly much. She was very used to being aware of spirit at the same time as listening to human talk. Then suddenly, she was riveted: the tall spirit standing by the plant at the window spoke. It was a teaching spirit, exuding a sense of mastery, and its words were usually brief and to the point—sometimes hilariously funny, although not always in a way that Char found amusing. Now it was saying simply, "Eva is your next apprentice." She sat up quite straight, screaming, "*What?*"

Christine stopped abruptly, alarmed. She looked round at the window, where Char was fixated, but could see nothing. Meanwhile Char had crumpled in the chair, her hands over her face, groaning. "No, no, you promised, you promised!" She paused to listen some more, then groaned again. "But I want my *life* back!" Then she shrugged, and laughed for a long time. Finally she stopped long enough to light herself a cigarette.

Christine, slightly miffed, grabbed her opportunity. "Do you mind telling me what that was about?"

"I'm sorry, I'm sorry, I just..." Char laughed ruefully. "I'm sorry, that was really rude. Spirit just told me that Eva is my next apprentice. Just when I thought I was free for a while! So I said, you *promised* I wouldn't have to have another private apprentice, and they said, no, we didn't, you just thought that. So then I said, I want my life back, and they said, Char, this *is* your life!"

She took a long drag on her cigarette, and leaned back, laughing and groaning at the same time.

Eva was in one of Char's classes and had had several readings with her over a period of years. The next morning, Char looked at her schedule and found that Eva had a half hour appointment with her. She shook her head, laughing. Should she tell her or should she not tell her? She decided she didn't need to think about that, all would be revealed shortly.

Eva was on time. As soon as she opened the door, Char could feel her nervousness, and hear the questions mulling in her head. While Eva sat down, Char said, "Hold on a minute, I gotta get coffee." The ludicrous nature of the situation was too much for her.

She went into the kitchen and tried to pull herself together, laughing hysterically into the coffee mug and slamming cupboard doors to cover the sounds. She always did manage to pull herself together for her clients and today was no exception. She went back in the front room and sat cross-legged on her chair the way she usually did, smiling at Eva's anxious face.

"OK, you wanna tell me what you are here for?"

Eva gulped. "Well, I wanna ask you about...about..." she looked down at her hands, knotted together in front of her "...teaching." She took a deep breath. Char chuckled quietly, and nodded.

"OK, well, does that mean you are interested in being a private apprentice?" She looked at Eva for confirmation, getting a nod of assent.

"If...well, if there is any possibility of that, yes, I guess I want to know what that means."

"A private apprenticeship is a big commitment, from you as well as from me. You really need to think about it for a couple of weeks, because you don't want to start in on it and then find it's too much for you. There are two basic ground rules: first, don't fuck with me!" She paused to laugh, a deep and slightly rueful belly laugh. "Second, do your homework…and you *will* be given homework!" She paused again, staring intently at Eva. She wanted to be sure she was being heard. Eva nodded.

"So that's the scoop. Let me know in a couple of weeks what you think. If you say yes, we'll start when it's time to start. Spirit will tell me that."

The ritual for Storme's graduation was attended by seventeen people, a mixture of friends and students. When the ceremonies were over, and all the giveaways had been distributed, there was a sumptuous feast cooked by one of Char's ex-students. As Char seized a brief moment to herself with a cigarette on the porch, a woman from one of her classes came out to sit with her.

"So…I hear that you've chosen Eva as your next apprentice."

Char clearly heard the unspoken words: *why didn't you choose me?* She laughed, saying, "No, *I* didn't choose her, I never choose my apprentices. Spirit just told me she was going to be my next apprentice, and that was that."

"Hmmm," Annette swirled the amber liquid in her glass, looking down at the patterns. Char waited for a moment, still feeling the unexpressed injury. Annette was jealous. It puzzled her. Why did Annette so strongly feel the need for a teacher? Did she see it as a hierarchy, and someone who became an apprentice as *better* than others?

"You know, some people just don't need a teacher, or at least they don't need *me* as their teacher. Teaching is a funny thing, you can't teach anyone something that they don't already know. All a teacher ever does is help to excavate the shit that is covering what a student already knows."

Annette looked up in surprise. "Excavate the shit?"

"Yes!" Char threw her head back and laughed. "That's really all I'm doing when I teach—I'm shoveling shit, and I'm trying to show someone how to do it themselves! I can't even do it for them, or at least in the long run there is absolutely no *point* in me doing it for them. And then, when they have learned how to do it themselves, they no longer need me." She turned to face Annette directly, with a broad smile. "So, I guess that's why spirit didn't send me you as an apprentice—you already know how to excavate your own shit!"

Eva was plunged into her new role as an apprentice with very little warning, when Char called to ask for help with Nancy, one of her longtime clients and more recent students.

Nancy had dark eyes and dark curly hair setting off her pale skin. A devotee of the Indian guru Amachi, she radiated a gentle warm presence. One morning when Char checked the phone messages before her first reading of the day, there was a call that made her frown. It was from Nancy's lover: "Char, I don't know when this will get to you—I hope you get it soon—I am really worried about Nancy, she's really losing it, and I don't know what to do. I was hoping you could give us some advice. If you can call us, that would be great. I guess she might be going to the mental hospital."

He left the number, so Char dialed it immediately, leaving a message on the machine. "Hi, Nancy, it's Char. I'm sorry you're feeling bad. If you need to see me, just come over whenever you can, I'll fit you in." That evening, Char was tidying the room after saying goodbye to her last client, when Nancy knocked at the door. She burst into sobs as Char invited her in. "Oh Char, I'm so relieved to see you, I just don't know what to do!"

Char held her soft body, shaking with sobs, and guided her to the sofa.

"Wait here, I'm going to call someone to come and help."

She dialed Eva's number, praying that she would be there. She was. "Eva! Can you come right over? I need your help."

She received an immediate assent. While she was waiting for Eva's arrival, she went into the kitchen and boiled some water for tea. She stood at the herbs shelf with her eyes closed waiting for instructions from spirit on what to brew, and then took down spearmint and chamomile. Humming a prayer, she added a teaspoonful of honey before she took it to her client, who was slumped on the sofa.

"Here, sweetie, this will help you until we can start the work. An ally will be here soon. Why don't you tell me what's going on?"

Nancy sat up and managed a weak smile as she sniffed. She took a sip of the hot liquid. With a sigh, she said, "I don't know what is going on, Char, I just don't know..." she sobbed once more, and Char went to sit beside her, putting her arm around the woman's shoulders. After a moment or two she began again. "I feel so homicidal...I guess that's the right word, I just want to kill everyone, and then, or maybe most of all, I want to kill myself. I don't know what it is, I feel like I'm going mad." She went limp. Char stroked her hair comfortingly, and got up. The pipe was calling her. She took it down off the shelf where it sat, and placed it on the coffee table, sitting cross-legged in front of it as she unwrapped its red leather cover. This was clearly some form of possession that required an exorcism, and she never normally would use the pipe in such a situation, but when it called, she always paid attention. She knew that it would instruct her in how to use it.

Nancy sighed again and rubbed her face with her hands. "I went to the mental hospital yesterday, but they were no help...I'm so afraid, Char, I'm afraid of what I will do. I keep getting these strange impulses surging through me to lash out, I don't know why, I don't know what at! I want to cut myself, it feels like that would help. I just want to feel a knife cutting through flesh." Her expression suddenly became wild, and she covered her face in her hands, holding her head as she rocked to and fro.

Char was silently praying as she laid the pipe out on the table. "Didn't your mother die recently?" she asked.

"Yes, two months ago…do you think this is to do with her?"

"It might be. She molested you when you were little, didn't she?"

Nancy nodded weakly, letting her hands fall into her lap.

"Well," said Char, getting up to fetch some matches, "when someone molests you, they get right inside you. This all makes sense. You have a little friend hanging out with you, and we need to not have that friend right now, so when Eva gets here to hold a space for you, we'll get rid of it. You're pretty weak—you've been dealing with this for a while—so I think it will be good to have someone who can just be your ally while my power animals and I do the work."

Eva walked in the door just then. Char introduced them. "I need you to hold a space for Nancy, so she will stay here and not go with whatever it is that is inside her, and also just hold her physically. You can hold her hands, or whatever works. Just make sure she doesn't hurt herself or someone else. She may want to roll around quite a lot—that's fairly common in situations like these. And pray really hard, OK?" She laughed her loud delighted laugh, that clearly said to any demons who might be present that they had better watch out. She made a small altar to one side, with things that called to her; some sage, a crystal and a couple of small rocks, a few feathers, a deer bone. Meanwhile, Eva lit candles on the shelves around the room, and moved a couple of chairs out of the way in case Nancy thrashed around.

Following Char's instructions, Nancy lay down on the floor with Eva sitting at her head, holding her hands. Char switched off the overhead light so that the room was filled with the erratic shadows of the candles, their bright flames piercing the darkness and sending a glow into the corners. Then she sat down and put the pipe together, pushing the small table out of the way. The herbs that she had been told to use lay in a plastic bag beside her. She took pinches of the mixture and pressed it into the bowl with her fingertips after offering it to each of the directions, praying out loud now, with an intense determination. Her deep breath drew the flame of the match downwards, as her lungs sucked and her mouth filled with smoke. Following the instructions she was being given by her spirit allies, she blew the smoke in the four directions and then into the body of the woman lying before her, all the time calling for a whole, congruent Nancy. Clouds of undefined bluey mist swam and floated around the three of them, eerie in the candlelight.

Char felt Raven taking over her body: feathers grew out of her all over until she felt completely covered, and scaly skin grew on the backs of her hands. When she felt the extension of the last feather from the tattoo on the back of her neck, she knew she was ready, iridescent and shiny. The woman on the floor began to jerk, and utter strange sounds. From the center of all the plumage, through the eyes of Raven, Char looked into Nancy's face, calling her name again and again, making a prayer out of the form she was calling to. She felt for Nancy, and only met the ugliness of the entity that had taken over, spitting and furious. She recognized it then as the negative aspects of the woman's mother, trying to live on in the body of the daughter they had once violated, knowing how to get inside her. Breathing steadily and calmly, knowing Raven all around her, she reached further in, and felt two minds, one the entity, and the other, weak and frightened, Nancy. The young woman's body was writhing as if trying to escape, but Eva had hold of her hands and although she rolled from one side to the other, she had to remain present. She howled intermittently, as she twisted this way and that. Occasionally Char would catch a glimpse of the face of the woman she was trying to access: terror distorted her features.

The entity had a strong hold and wasn't going to depart easily. Char felt its rage, a swirling blackness trying to engulf her as it had engulfed Nancy. Then she heard her voice through Raven's beak, speaking reassuring words, lulling the entity into a sense of security. Nancy's howls quieted, and Raven reached into her ribcage with its talons, getting a grip before the demon could realize what was happening. All of a sudden, a look of pure rage came over Nancy, and she opened her eyes wide, staring directly into Char's. In that moment Char felt the entity's desire to kill her, and she was very glad that Eva had hold of the woman. Putting her face close to Nancy's mouth, she started sucking. She found she had a piece of sage and a pebble in her own mouth, and realized she must have picked them up off the altar without even knowing what she was doing. She sucked and sucked, as Raven held the energy, until she felt her mouth fill with the energy of the entity, contained in the sage and the pebble. Then it was done, and Nancy went limp. Char put the sage and the pebble carefully to one side—she would get rid of them later. She did a little more healing, soothing the ragged places in Nancy's battered aura, but the most important part of the work was clearly over. Soon she was sitting up. The tears of desperation were replaced with tears of gratitude.

A few days later, Nancy came by for a quick check-in. Though still a little weary, she was recovering fast. Char was pleased. "You need to realize that you are stronger than any external entity that might try to take you over," she told her.

Nancy shook her head, uncertainly. "I wish I could believe that, but I didn't feel like I could do anything about what was happening. I felt like it had complete power over me."

Char smiled, her head on one side. "You found your way to me, didn't you? You are much stronger than you think you are. One day you will be doing this kind of work. What you just went through was a kind of shamanic break, an experience you needed to go through to prepare yourself to be a healer. It takes nothing less than everything to be a good healer. Your 'everything' is being called forth."

Char's blue eyes met Nancy's brown ones and held for a moment. Then Char broke into peals of laughter, and they hugged each other with fierce warmth.

Chapter Thirteen

Joy had been doing psychic readings for some years when she first met Char, who was working in the San Francisco Bay Area at the time. A friend had called to say, "I've met this amazing shaman! I told her about you and your background in doing ceremonial work, and she asked if you would like to come and help with a house blessing, since she lives in Seattle and all her normal helpers are up there."

So Joy showed up and was sitting in the living room, when a whirlwind blew in: a dramatic little person with lots of bird energy, and intense bright power radiating out from her lithe physical form. As soon as introductions were over, Char addressed Joy with her usual brilliant smile:

"I hear you can go out into other realms?"

"Yes, I can."

Char nodded, "Well, go out then. If you see anything let me know." She promptly launched into the house blessing.

Given permission, Joy sat in a chair and did a psychic scan during the work. Char had it well under control, but Joy was able to help by pointing out a couple of strange pieces of stray energy that were trying to hide in corners. She watched with interest as Char transformed into a being that walked with absolute clarity and presence on the other side, in another dimension. Listening to her sing a sleep song over the bed, she was very stirred by Char's ability to use sound to transform energy, not just because her singing voice is lovely, but because the Lakota chant itself was so evocative of peace and harmony. What impressed her most was how Char did the work gently rather than fiercely. Her approach was deeply compassionate towards the troubled spirits that she was dealing with, and she was always willing to negotiate with them, yet she stuck to her commitment to make the place clean for the person who occupied it. Later they both laughed at the things they saw that were invisible to most people: at one point, the energies she was removing had the form of a herd of pygmy rhinoceros.

Lena, Joy's partner, had lived in a cave in the Himalayas for seven years, studying Buddhism with a Tibetan teacher, and she was just as extraordinary as such a history would lead one to presume. When she first met Char she was enchanted by her aura, which was a light gold color, full of constantly dancing sparkling motes, like dust motes in a sunbeam, as though she was surrounded by many microscopic little fairies. As time passed, Lena noticed that it was slightly less brilliant when Char was tired, but it never ceased its constant dancing. She was not at all surprised to hear that Char had chosen Sundust as her last name.

Lena thought of Char as a *tulkuth*: a person who is raised from a young age to be a shaman or a priest, or a power entity of some kind. It was a concept she had learned from the Tibetan culture, where it is common to recognize a child with unusual potential while he or she is still very young. Such a child is taught that she is greater than others, therefore responsible for them to some degree, and expected to act more responsibly. She never has to vie in the schoolyard for her status like the rest of the kids; it is simply assumed. That's a hard thing to do to a kid, since she won't be able to find peers who can be her friends. She is inevitably in danger of great loneliness, often leading to hubris. Lena saw Char as lonely, certainly—but she had somehow avoided the hubris part.

Because she is a tulkuth, everyone wants a piece of Char, and a great part of her training, especially with Keith, had informed her that she was not to resist giving herself. She was forbidden to set limits; her job was to be there for others whenever they needed her. In the Tibetan culture, she would have taken vows to that effect, but there would be servants around to set limits for her, and the people who came for help would understand that they needed to bring a gift in exchange for the energy the tulkuth gave them. In the West, none of that is understood, and it is much more likely that someone with Char's gifts will be drained dry at a young age.

In spite of Char's obvious skill, and her unmistakable power, both Joy and Lena saw the vulnerable woman who was sometimes young, tired and fragile, and they gravitated towards taking care of her. They were appalled by the number of people who seemed to see her as consumer goods, who were looking for something outside of themselves, and wanted to bask in the reflected light; people who didn't realize that they can learn to do their own magic. Joy felt very maternal towards her. Her daughter Ronnie kept her distance to begin with, in typical teenage fashion, though she was soon won over by Char's irresistible charm, and, over time, saw her as an elder sister.

It was absolutely new for Char to find people who chose to take care of her instead of taking from her. To begin with she didn't believe it, but as time passed, she realized they were very genuine in their offers, and she accepted gratefully. She had always been suspicious of white people who did psychic work, since her experience was that they were on power trips, and that was also what Keith had specifically taught her. But Joy and Lena were clearly women of integrity. They assisted her in recharging her own batteries so she could do her work more effectively. Both of them had worked in the same kinds of arenas, and understood about re-arranging energies, so they were able to give some useful advice about tapping into universal energy when Char needed it, instead of calling on her own personal resources. Spending a lot of time on other planes inevitably meant that Char sometimes ceased to be grounded in the physical world, and there was a vital need for her to balance her presence in the different realms, to bring her focus one hundred percent back to the physical. Joy and Lena helped her to remember to be fully present in the here and now. They provided her with three square meals a day, making sure she ate them. Char had a tendency to forgo food when she was overly stressed with her work, or with any intense emotion, and she also wasn't immune to the typical Westerner's fear of getting fat. That cut no ice with Lena, an excellent cook who loved to feed her friends.

For a week or so every two months, when she was in the San Francisco Bay Area, Char worked out of their house. That meant a house filled with power animals, and shimmering with Char's unique energy. It was a little chaotic, since many things in many realms, including the physical, were moved around and sometimes left in strange places. But Char's pervasive, bouncy charm was always delightful.

Even when they were not in a work situation, Char could and would immediately step over into other realms if she perceived a need. When Joy was out there with her, she saw Char as separate from her power animals, although they seemed to share a locus point. There were two overlapping glows, distinct from each other even though they coexisted within the same sphere. In ordinary reality, Joy found her eyes did not have the depth perception to see them as separate beings, and she was occasionally startled to see Snow Leopard obscuring the physical manifestation that was Char.

Joy had previously trained in Tibetan Bon shamanism, which has its own system but uses many of the same elements. She saw Char's method as more accessible to non-Tibetan Buddhists, since the Bon practices involve a lot of Sanskrit and Tibetan chants. They did a series of soul retrievals together. Soon Char was directing Joy to do the extractions, or the retrieval part, or the ancestral part. They found that, whereas Char worked most easily with heart issues, Joy worked well with ancestral issues. During the work, they seemed to share perceptions, and were able to remain aware of each other, without having a mental dialogue. Both understood how to operate in the slippery realities of realms outside our ordinary, everyday reality. Joy had some training in Jungian therapy, and she understood the Western concept of those realms as the different levels of the collective unconscious, where archetypes exist. As she became familiar with power animals, she understood them to be archetypes, rather than consciousness. They would respond to the needs of the people present, but had no volition of their own. With Char's assistance, Joy discovered that Bear was her primary power animal, and it would come up over her, enfolding her from behind. Cobra was another strong medicine for her, that also seemed to come up from behind, like someone known and well loved wrapping her in a blanket. They performed very different functions: Bear was sheer energy, ruthless, fierce and fearless. It would do whatever was necessary without judgment, quite unattached to outcome—very appropriate for the animal that sits in the West. Cobra was subtler, complementary to Char's bird energy. It would turn up to deal with negative energy that had solidified in a person's subtler channels, softening and loosening it, so that it could be pulled out without creating trauma. Some intrusions have wispy tendrils that become entwined, so that ripping them out would be undesirable.

As she did more of the work, Joy began to see a client's life-force as a matrix, and Char showed her how to replace parts, such as an unhealthy liver, with parts brought back from an earlier time, when the body was still healthy. If the client was ready to accept health (*re-member* it), then the new part slipped easily into the matrix. She learned how the archetypes that turned up to assist are always relevant to the client, often very specifically so. She might see a tall woman in red and white wielding a sword, that the client would immediately recognize as a childhood heroine. Other archetypes were more generic, like a pillar of fire or a female presence. Either way, those archetypes were like power animals—a powerful source of regenerative and protective energy, always available to the client.

Lena knew some of the archetypes that turned up. Kali, also known as Durga, was one of the Hindu goddesses she had become very familiar with when she was living in the Himalayas. In spite of this, she didn't choose to learn how to do this kind of healing work. "I don't believe that everything is for the ultimate good like Char does," she explained. "She trusts that we are guided by spirit and that spirit knows best, that spirit knows when you should do something and when you should not. It works for Char to believe that there is a captain steering the ship, and it doesn't work for me. I think to do this particular kind of healing, you need to have that trust."

Nevertheless, Lena had a great regard for Char's work. She saw how easily Char worked magic, how she was able to move matter without using her muscles, a skill she assumed that Char learned when she was very young, when her mother was suffering from debilitating depressions that made it imperative for Char to take charge. She also admired how Char inspired immediate love and trust in most of the people she met. "It's partly that she is naturally a very openhearted person, but it's also a thing she does with her aura," she said, adding in a less happy tone, "Sometimes I want to put a cork in her generosity, because some days there isn't anything left to give!"

Since Lena was a very concrete sort of person, her role in Char's work was primarily staying in her body, keeping a focus in the physical, so that those who were *out there* would have a clearly marked place to come back to. It was a conscious decision for her not to put her attention on the other side, but to watch, does the fire need wood, is someone at the door? When someone else was holding ground, and she did look over *there*, she would see Char running along the plains of the other side in cat form, or bird form. She always knew which one was Char, because the same sparkles were in her aura on the other side too. She saw Char removing intrusions by simply unhooking them from where they were attached by karmic lines, so that they would go sliding down their future. What she perceived were not entities, but clumps of energy, animated but not alive, not possessing any life force of their own. They looked like mice or rats to her, though she understood that was only a cartoon animation that allowed her to perceive them. Occasionally she would see the cats pouncing on them as Char threw them aside, if they didn't immediately disappear out of the window.

As I talked with Joy and Lena, I understood how differently people may see, and therefore label, an image in other realms, even when they are seeing essentially the same thing, something that is composed of the same essential energy. Everything is energy, in different forms. Our imagery—the personal symbols that we are inspired to use to put a name to a particular kind of energy—is very individual. Joy, Lena and Char might all see the same thing occurring in another realm, yet they might describe it quite differently. However, when they are all focused on the same objective, they would all share the same interpretation of effect and intent.

After witnessing clients whose defense mechanisms melted as their old belief systems changed, Joy and Lena both chose to have their own soul retrievals. Lena cackled like an insane waterfowl while Char was working on her, because it felt funny and hurt a lot. She is the kind of person who would want to kill someone who was cutting her open and removing things, and laughter was an outlet for some of the restraint that was necessary in order for her to allow Char to do the work. At one point she had her allies sit on her hands and feet, because she wasn't sure she would successfully refrain from hitting Char.

She chose to have the soul retrieval because of metabolic problems which she was pretty sure had a psychological and spiritual basis. Afterwards, she felt like everything was in disarray, as though Char had been through her looking for something, which indeed she had.

Coyote was Lena's primary power animal. Char introduced her to Otter, who taught her how to play, and then to Moose, who taught her to walk lightly and gently, floating silently in the mist in spite of physical or metaphorical size. Lena also learned other things; being the rebellious soul she is, when Char said not to talk to things with teeth while you are journeying on the other side, Lena thought, "Why not?" When she saw something with teeth, she talked to it. She soon found that it wouldn't leave her alone, and it quickly got nasty. Now, not wishing to invite harassment, she is more discerning.

Char was rarely ill, but a day did occur when she felt very sick. As she lay on the bed with Lena—who is an acupuncturist—sticking needles in her, Lena said, "Char, I don't think you are going to be well enough to do a soul retrieval this afternoon."

Char opened her aching eyes to say, "Yes, I will."

Lena felt on her knee for a point, prior to inserting a needle. "Hmmmm," she intoned, in a way that presaged an important statement, "Well, I don't think you should push yourself. I believe the woman who is coming is a client of Joy's and knows her well, so why don't you ask Joy if she will do the work?"

Char opened her eyes again and sighed with pain. She considered for a moment. Then she said, "OK! Spirit says its fine. Joy is certainly good enough to do it." The retrieval went well, and Char slept all the way through it. From then on, Joy did that kind of work freely, taking some of the load off Char.

Whenever Char stayed in the San Francisco Bay Area, she led a drum journey that was open to the public. Drum journeying is an excellent tool for accessing information that sometimes can't be accessed in the physical world. As always when she was organizing something, Char followed spirit's instructions, and today she was looking for Joy's daughter to help her.

"Where's Ronnie?' Char poked her head into the study where Joy and Lena sat.

"I expect she's downstairs," answered Joy. "Probably working on her computer."

Char disappeared, reappearing a few minutes later to confer with Ronnie in one corner of the room. Then Char came into the study for a cigarette, while Ronnie went out into the garden. She came back in with a handful of small rocks, which she placed on the bathroom counter, closing the bathroom door behind her. Soon I heard the sound of a hairdryer, and Joy, standing beside me as I was making a cup of tea, laughed out loud. Shortly, the drone of the hair dryer stopped, and Joy called into the bathroom, "Ronnie, have you been blow-drying rocks?"

There was a slight pause, then Ronnie poked her face out, and with a hint of amusement in her voice, she replied, "Yes! They were wet and I wanted to dry them. How did you know?"

Joy laughed. "I could feel the rocks, they thought it was very odd!"

Later, we all sat in a circle in the living room, along with five newcomers who had come to journey. In the center, unceremoniously placed on the floor, were four small rocks forming a tiny altar, with a larger rock in the center. Each of the directions had a piece of paper to mark it. The paper in the East said: Air, hawk, change, new beginnings. South said: mouse, buffalo, passion, fire, innocence. West said: going within, water, emotions, movement within. North said: wisdom, the grandmothers, earth, the darkness.

When we were all silent, Char prayed to the seven directions (the center, above, and below, as well as the four we all know), using her rattle, calling in all that is good, true, and beautiful. When she was done, she talked to us about a drum journey. "I haven't done exactly this before, spirit told me to do it this way. What you are going to do is look around the room and each of you will find a rock sitting on a shelf or a table, just somewhere around, and each rock will have one of the directions written on it. It's the issues relative to this direction that you need to be dealing with right now, and when you journey you will get information that is relevant to these issues. OK?" We all nodded, and she laughed. "OK, go find your rock! And you are not allowed to take one off the altar!"

I glanced behind me and saw a little white rock on a shelf. When I picked it up, I found that it had the letter N on it. That suited me: I like North. Other people were still looking for their rocks. After five minutes, when Cindy had still not found one, Char negotiated to give her one off the altar.

"OK, is everyone ready?" asked Char. " Now we are going to go round and I want everyone to say briefly what their direction is and what it means to them, what issues they see as being relevant to them."

Myrna was on her left, so she began. "Well, I have a red rock, and it has West on it. So what this says to me is that I need to be following the practices of the good red road, and I need to be looking within myself to access the inner voice so that I can know what practices are right for me. I need to just sit with myself. I know that's important, but it's not easy for me." She looked at Char, and their faces both crinkled in laughter at the inevitable recurrence of Myrna's ongoing theme. There was something so sweet about the way Char smiles, it almost made me want to cry. I felt her love as a tangible force in the circle, supporting us all as we did this work.

One by one we went around, and when that was done, Char picked up the drum, stroking its face gently with her right hand. Because she came here by plane, she hadn't brought her own drum, and she was using mine. I liked to see it being used by her.

Char began to talk about how to journey. "Everyone here has a couple of power animals, right? At least one, anyway? So this time I want you all to go in a canoe, and your feminine ancestors will be on the left, and your masculine on the right, only the ones that are here for the good, true, and the beautiful. Your power animals will be there too, guiding and protecting you, one in the front and one in the back. There are a couple of people who have never journeyed before, am I right?" She glanced around, and two people raised their hands. "OK, so just to let you know when it is time to come back I will do this kind of beat." She hit the drum slowly six or seven times. "When you hear that sound it means you have to get back in the canoe wherever you are, and come home. You will have about a minute to get home, back to this everyday reality. Then you might want to write down where you have been and what you experienced. It's easy to forget, so everyone should have pen and paper beside them.

"I want you to ask yourselves the following questions: Is something preventing you from having or doing or expressing the quality of the direction you have been given? What one thing needs to happen to bring this quality into consciousness and bring it into the present? What kind of plan do you need to bring it into the present and how will you take this plan into action?" She paused and looked round at us all searchingly. "OK? Has everyone got it? These are the questions you are going to take with you. You are journeying to find the answers. You might meet all kinds of beings on your travels, and it's OK to ask them if they know the answers to these questions. If they have any information for you, they will probably give it to you, but you can always ask more than once. The only thing is you should avoid any creature that has nasty looking teeth. Hopefully you won't meet any, but if you do, just go the other way—don't engage with them. You don't have to talk to any being you don't want to. Is that clear?"

A few people asked for clarification and Char talked a little more. Then she stood up, and we all lay down or sat, making ourselves comfortable and closing our eyes, getting ourselves ready to journey. Char took the drumstick in her right hand and tapped the drum once. Then she began to hit it regularly and fast, so that the sound filled the room.

At first I tried to imagine the canoe: I saw myself sitting in it with my snake up front, looking over the bow, and my cat behind. Then I quickly found that the cat didn't want to go in the water, and my horse wanted to accompany us, but wouldn't fit in the canoe, so I gave it up, and let myself spiral into infinity with the sound of the drum, the way I normally did, grateful that journeying happened so easily for me. I felt the wisdom of the North coursing through my veins, and I saw the ancient Grandmothers sitting in circle. I became the network of life itself, the thread that runs through everything. In this amorphous state I examined the world for while, until I had the sensation of dissolving completely and becoming pure spirit. I floated until I felt the need to be more grounded, then I became my snake and crawled around the room looking at everyone. All too soon, the drum sound changed: it was time to return to the here and now. I pulled myself back into my body, opened my eyes and started to write about my journey. I heard others stirring around me and glanced up. Char was sitting by the fireplace, the drum at her side, her head resting on her knee. Catching my eye, she grinned widely.

When it seemed like we were all finished, or nearly finished writing, she sat up straight and spoke. "OK, when you are ready I want you all to find a partner, and share with each other what your journey was like and what were the answers, or the answer, that you received. The job of the person listening is simply to listen without comment and then when you have finished talking she will give you feedback, maybe pointing out areas where she heard something that you didn't, or where she sees something that you have missed. Then when we have all shared with a partner, we will go round and share in the whole group. Please notice whoever is opposite you, because whatever that person says is likely to be very relevant to you, or at least to your power nature; that is, whatever it is that you need in order to claim your power."

We began to get into couples. Most of us were allowed to choose our own partner freely but Char took me by the arm and steered me towards Cindy. "I want you two to be partners, OK?" She smiled at us, with her eyebrows raised in a way that might have been a question, but really wasn't. I figured spirit had probably told her we were to be together, so that's the way it would be. I sat down on the sofa while Cindy sat on the floor in front of me, and I told her my journey. She listened patiently, and then looked at me and said, "That sounds like you! I especially like the bit about you being the thread that ties everything together. That seems like it would be important to you. And then being the snake—that was cool."

I nodded, smiling. "Yes, it was cool. It was a big snake, but she couldn't quite get up on everything. She tried to get up on the table and couldn't quite make it. That's not the first time I have become one of my power animals. I've been a big cat running in the forest once—that was amazing."

We smiled at each other, and she picked up the notes that lay on the floor in front of her.

"I tried going in the canoe too, and it didn't work for me either. So I just let myself go to this place that I often go in meditations. It's a plateau overlooking a canyon, like the Grand Canyon, a desert landscape. My power animals are Buffalo, Mouse and Dove, and they were all there. This time Buffalo talked to me. He said, 'Get your house in order, and let go of unnecessary people that will stop you from being who you are.' He told me I had the wrong stone, and the funny thing is that as soon as I lay down I found I had lost my stone anyway. But he told me I always have the right stone, and this is it!" She showed me a beautiful amethyst carved in the form of an ancient goddess, which she was wearing around her neck. "He said I was to let go of my pain. I don't need to hold onto old pain. What stops me from being in the present is fear of what people will think, and also fear of being hounded by people who want something from me. I have basic survival fears that I need to deal with.

"Buffalo had little bits of steam coming out of his nose, and his nose was so soft—he let me touch it, and it was like spirit's nose. It represents the softness that I need to allow people to see in myself, when I'm free of the fear that they will judge me as weak and insecure. He said that when I touch his nose there is no fear, and I should remember how sweet the feeling is in my hand and in my heart. It's what others will see in me and if I remember that, I can be in the present."

She paused, turning over the piece of paper in her hand. I waited, knowing there was more and eager to hear it.

"Hmm...there is some other stuff but I don't know whether he said it, or whether I just heard it, if you know what I mean...these were the words: 'Listen to the water. There are many suns, they are all beautiful. Look to each one as powerful and healing. Feel the warmth of Father Sky.'"

Char had been crawling around the room from couple to couple, listening to what was being said, and she heard Cindy's last few sentences. She smiled at us, laughed a little, and carried on to the next couple.

Cindy looked up at me, and I realized she was done. I said, "Wow! That all sounds very amazing! Good information! Useful for me too, that stuff about being soft and vulnerable. You really travel. That is so cool that you can go to that plateau, and it sounds like a great place. And that is so neat that you can remember exactly what the touch of his nose was like. "

When it was time to go around the circle, we shared, and then listened to others. One of the two women opposite us was talking about seeing spiders on her journey. "They were all sizes and I felt really creeped out by them, so I tried to go the other way, but my power animal, which is a fox, was eating some of them! Afterwards, when I told my partner about this—" she grinned sideways at the woman sitting next to her "—she asked me if it had ever occurred to me that spiders could be food, and I could just eat the ones that I want, and ignore the rest. I don't have to alter my path to avoid them! I never had thought of it that way, so that was really good info for me to hear." She carried on talking but I had reached the limit of my ability to take in information. Later, however, Char came up to me and Cindy as we were getting ready to leave, and said, "Did you both hear that stuff about the spiders, and her being able to eat the ones she chose?" We nodded. "Well, that's important information for both of you. Spirit said I should tell you!" She crinkled her eyes with joyful laughter and we hugged good night.

The following day we did Joy's soul retrieval. Joy is an intense kind of person and I knew her soul retrieval would be intense. We all settled ourselves in the living room, while Joy talked for a while about the changes she wanted to make: getting rid of old guilt that she felt was holding her back from her full potential, and regaining her health. Her mother had died an invalid, and Joy was realistically alarmed at how much her own health mirrored her mother's. She wanted her good knees from before she had her motorbike accident. She wanted a return of her vitality and energy, which had steadily gone down the drain in the last few years.

When she had finished speaking, Char went round the circle of allies, asking each of us what we wanted for Joy. That was not something she normally did, but I knew she felt that Joy could handle any input that came forth. I had been quite moved at how Joy had articulated herself so I shrugged with a grin, saying, "I am really impressed with what you said. It sounds great to me!"

Char looked at Ronnie, who was next to me, leaning forward with her elbows on her knees. "I want Mom to have more of a sense of humor," she said decisively.

Joy looked surprised. "I *do* have a sense of humor!"

"Not when something goes wrong, you always take it really seriously. I want you to be able to laugh when things go wrong. Just make a joke out of it." Ronnie talked like her mother, very sure of herself.

Joy shrugged. Char glanced at her, and nodded. She turned to Lena, Joy's lover of thirteen years. "I want Joy to stop saying she's sorry," said Lena. "I will ask her a perfectly simple question, like where is the towel, and she will reply, 'I'm sorry.' That isn't helpful to me at all. I just want to know where the towels are!"

Joy interjected, "Well, that's part of my guilt stuff."

Lena nodded. "Yes, you always take responsibility for everything, you think everything is your fault, even when it is nothing to do with you. I'm not saying you stole the towel! I just want to be able to ask without feeling like I have to be careful how I phrase what I ask so that you will feel OK about it. Sometimes I am fierce about things and I want that to be OK."

Joy smiled affectionately at her partner. "Well, I love your fierceness, and I want you to be fierce!"

Char looked up from scribbling in her notebook, and said, "OK, well, I'll see what I can do. It sounds to me like you two have taken little bits of each other, which often happens in relationships, and that may well turn up in the work."

I found myself thinking that if Joy was really able to make these changes after the soul retrieval, then Char will have done some truly remarkable work. It seemed such a basic part of who Joy was, that she said she was sorry for things not her responsibility.

Char put her pen down and stood up, stretching her arms above her head. She dropped her arms, buried her head in her chest for a moment, then said thoughtfully, "Spirit is saying I should do this soul retrieval sitting up. Let's just put Joy's chair in the middle of the room."

Everyone meandered around, getting prepared for the event. Finally Joy was ensconced in the chair, and Char was sitting on a stool in front of her, head bent on her knees, arms around her legs. Myrna and Ronnie sat on the sofa, while Lena was beside Joy. I was behind her with the drum, carefully avoiding the pathway to the window that Char would use to get rid of whatever was extracted. Char glanced up to nod at me, and I began, the beat of the drum singing to us as it filled the room.

Soon Char sat up straight, making the sound of a raven, a raucous caw. She reached forward with a claw-like hand to grab something out of Joy's chest, sweeping it away in graceful curves. She bent forward again, her head down, but soon she was bouncing on two feet, like a bird, around to Joy's back. Joy leaned forward, and Char symbolically cut her open with the Tibetan knife that Lena had given her, to remove more gunk. That done, she bounced back around to the front of the chair and put her arm over Joy's knee, letting her head drop. Her wild red hair—as fine as feathers and grown below her shoulders in the three years that I had known her—hid her face, and then she turned her head to the side so that we could hardly tell where her face was. There was a long pause and I concentrated on the regular fast beat. Suddenly Char turned back towards Joy, and using both hands she dug into Joy's belly, urgently reaching inwards until she got a hold of something and pulled it out slowly and steadily, hand over hand, wrapping it up before she threw it away. She ignored Joy's jerks and grunts of pain and I wondered if she could even see or hear them. She turned back to crouch by Joy's knee again, and then reached behind for the pen, laying herself on the floor to write some brief scribbles on the pad that sat by Ronnie's feet. Now she bounced to the back of Joy again and pulled out more stuff from around her neck. Then she reached forward with both hands to remove something tenacious and wriggly from Joy's face. She had already ripped off her sweater from the heat of the work, and I saw the muscles of her forearm quivering with effort. Joy laughed out loud, grinning broadly at Lena sitting beside her.

Char settled herself next to Joy's knee again for a while, cawing occasionally. Twice she reached towards Lena to grab something from her throat and chest. Once she reached back to Ronnie and pulled something out of her. It seemed like the work went on forever, and I reminded myself that I always forget the passage of time. Fortunately my drum seemed to drum itself. A couple of times I found myself humming, and I stopped myself, in case it would distract Char from her journeying, though it seemed too quiet a sound to carry over the thud of the drum. At last, tossing the hair away from her face, she looked at me and used her finger to slice across her throat. I dropped the drumstick to my side, recognizing her sign for *cut*. She took the crystal she had been holding, that stored the parts she brought back, and blew through it four times into Joy's heart area, and then into her head. She moved on and blew twice into Lena's head, and finally Ronnie's, returning parts they had lost in typical family dynamics, where things become a little more interwoven than they should be. Later they both told me they experienced a *hunk*, neither heard nor felt by the rest of us, and places that they had not been aware of as not-quite-solid, suddenly became more solid.

She stood up at last, smiled lovingly, and said, "There you are, darlin', it's done!"

Joy grinned up at her. "Thank you so much, sweetheart!" Then she frowned, looking past Char's head, saying, "I think you should have Myrna clean you off, it looks like you've got some schmutz on you."

They stepped into a corner, and Myrna stood in front of her, growling a little, as her hands formed into claws, and she pulled something off Char's hair, tossing it towards the window. She took the rattle and shook it around the medicine woman's head before she would allow her to go outside to smoke.

I made myself a cup of tea. Myrna walked by me and stopped, looking at my shoulder. "You have something on you too!" she said. She made a slow scooping motion with one hand, gracefully sweeping away whatever it was she saw, which was unseen by me. Then she turned me around, looked me over, and stepped away, smiling. "OK, you're all cleaned up!"

When Char came back in, she put her arm around my shoulders, saying, "That was great drumming, and the chanting was wonderful too. Thank you so much!"

I looked at her in surprise. "I was chanting?"

She nodded, grinning. "You didn't know?"

"I hummed a couple of times, but I didn't think I was chanting. Are you sure it was me?"

"It came from the direction of the drum. Maybe it was your power animals!"

I lay on the floor in the living room while Char told Joy what she had seen and done. Their voices flowed in and out of my consciousness. I was only fully aware of the atmosphere of love in the room, which cloaked its inhabitants in a peaceful warmth. Somehow, in spite of my initial doubt, I knew that Joy would be giving up her incessant need to apologize.

Author bio: **MIKAYA HEART** has studied various forms of shamanism, and journeyed to many places, in many different realms. A writer, a mystic, and a teacher, she has an unswerving commitment to honoring the Earth and living fully. She grew up in Scotland and is now based in rural California.

LaVergne, TN USA
30 October 2009
162527LV00004B/10/P